James Simmons

POEMS 1956-1986

POEMS
1956-1986

Introduced by Edna Longley

Gallery Books

BLOODAXE BOOKS

Poems 1956-1986
is first published
simultaneously in paperback
and in a clothbound edition
in November 1986 by

The Gallery Press / Peter Fallon
19 Oakdown Road
Dublin 14, Ireland

and, in England,
Scotland and Wales, by

Bloodaxe Books Ltd.
P.O. Box 1SN
Newcastle upon Tyne NE99 1SN
England.

ISBN 1 85235 002 4 Gallery Books (*paperback*)
1 85235 003 2 Gallery Books (*clothbound*)
1 85224 020 2 Bloodaxe Books (*paperback*)
1 85224 019 9 Bloodaxe Books (*clothbound*)

Grateful acknowledgement is made to Anne Tannahill and The Blackstaff Press, Belfast, for permission to include poems from *From the Irish* (1985).

Requests to use the poems in this collection in anthologies *et cetera* should be addressed to The Gallery Press.

The Gallery Press receives financial assistance from An Chomhairle Ealaíon / The Arts Council, Ireland.

Bloodaxe Books Ltd. acknowledges the financial assistance of Northern Arts.

The publishers acknowledge the assistance of The Arts Council of Northern Ireland in the publication of this book.

Contents

Introduction

In the poetry of James Simmons art and life never look like becoming polite strangers. Their intimacy declares itself through the effortlessly natural tones of the poet's voice – at once source and focus of the pervasive vitality. Whether lyrical or plainspoken, confiding or confessional, pointing a moral or telling a tale, the poems have an air of very immediately addressing the reader out of the immediacy of experience. Simmons's theory, too, favours direct methods that connect on a live fuse the poet, his subject matter and his audience. In the sequence 'No Land is Waste'* he argues, in a suitably demotic idiom, for a democracy of the imagination as opposed to the remote, aristocratic stance of T. S. Eliot:

> The pompous swine . . .
> that man's not hollow, he's a mate of mine.

Simmons's other and inseparable career as songwriter and singer both explains and sustains such an aesthetic. 'Didn't He Ramble', a tribute to jazz, affirms the origins of the artist's words and music in the tribe and its unpurified dialect:

> the word of life, if such a thing existed,
> was there on record among the rubbish listed
> in the catalogues of Brunswick and H.M.V.,
> healing the split in sensibility.
> Tough reasonableness and lyric grace
> together, in poor man's dialect.
> Something that no one taught us to expect.
> Profundity without the po-face
> of court and bourgeois modes. This I could use
> to live and die with. Jazz. Blues.

**The Keepsake Press, Surrey*, 1972

Although Simmons's range encompasses many 'classical' effects, his commitment to 'the word of life', as a touchstone for style and content, makes him one in spirit with these jazzmen. If we grant the term its full weight, he is a 'folksinger' in his poetry as he is a poet in his songs.

Simmons's 'word of life', however, does not confine itself to the good news. In 'Me and the World' he personifies the world as an unpredictable lover, often 'estranged by flaws of mine or withdrawn/for her own reasons'; while in 'A Muse' inspiration itself assumes the same fickle guise: 'Her/charm is in being chancy'. The special immediacy of Simmons's poetry also derives from its authenticity as the fluctuating response of a representatively 'flawed' individual to a 'chancy' universe. And the rough course of true – or untrue – love is central to the plot of the continuing drama thus established:

> If our luck should run out
> and love withers and dies, love,
> don't try out of kindness
> to save me with lies, love.
> You won't need to explain
> that I'm single again
> and the marriage is done
> when your kiss says goodbye.

That stanza, from 'The Silent Marriage', epitomises and holds in a rare poise the conflicts in Simmons's perception of love, and perhaps of life: ecstatic moments, all-too-probable decline or betrayal, the incompatibility of passion with permanence, a slightly over-optimistic faith in the resolving power of honesty. Similar perspectives condition his larger exploration of the tensions between romance and domesticity, freedom and responsibility, youth and age. Simmons has taken some highly unflattering 'photographs' of marriage, which attempt to fix the reality beneath the 'Arcadian' mask: 'my wife/and I are never glaring/in photographs'. But time, in traditional manner, is seen as the ultimate betrayer of idylls and ideals:

for I
who loved Illona Massey at fourteen
with a great love am now a has-been.
(For John Clare)

Perhaps never, or only when drunk, does life
seem as it once seemed, a war to be won.
The moving and influential things they devised
have all been said and done, it seems, by others.
Some do the very things that they despised
and recognise the enemy as brothers. . .
(Sonnet for the Class of '58)

This needling consciousness of how time and ties can devour the free spirit instals the Ulysses myth as a subterranean point of reference in Simmons's poetry. It eventually surfaces in 'On Circe's Island', but many other poems conjure up the liberating sea, voyages of discovery, the thrill of an exotic landfall:

the shape of an inlet
where long-boats scraped
ashore, the look of a cape
round which is Durban.
(The Straight Line and the Circle)

Yet Simmons, like Ulysses, tends to come round full circle, to the full complexities, as do the restless pioneers in 'Ballad of New Frontiers', finally 'Aware of sounds we'd heard before/off Boston on the Eastern shore'. The complexities, including death – that inescapable destination and commitment – are most completely felt in his *King Lear* sequence, which also incorporates Simmons's most completely developed mythological framework. He sets up camp on the edge of 'the wilderness' and of Shakespeare, and, partly by mocking the pretension of both these actions, holds up perhaps his largest and clearest mirror to the mortal predicament:

Two campers (King Lear and his clown?)
smile to see the skies come down.
The shaken mind finds metaphors
in winds that shake the great outdoors.
As roofs and fences fall in storms
the tranquil mind's protective forms
collapse when passion, grief and fear
stir. We will spend a fortnight here.
(Outward Bound)

Simmons's flirtations with Shakespearean drama draw attention to the variety of his own *dramatis personae*. He generally plays the lead himself, of course, his voice modulating to express different moods and attitudes, from anger, lust and jealousy to tenderness, humour and satire. 'Written, Directed by and Starring . . .', a fine example of Simmons's ironic mask, can be read as a gloss on such self-dramatisation, and on the way in which his 'scripts' have kept pace with the changing stage of his world:

The hero never hogs the screen because
his wife, his children, friends, events intrude.
When he's not on the story doesn't pause –
not if he dies. I don't see why it should.

Wife, children, friends and lovers are only some of the characters who crowd the screen. Many others take their bow in this densely populated poetry: shell-shocked 'Uncle Jack', a chain-smoking professor, an 'Old Gardener', the bizarre celluloid figures of 'Summer Lightning', writers and the characters *they* have created, idolised entertainers. Simmons the director often commends members of his cast for the zest with which they throw themselves into their roles, for their mastery of technical skills:

And even when I'd heard the stories
time and time before,

I loved them for the style
and for the way he held the floor,

one foot upon the hearth, one elbow
on the mantelpiece . . .
(Ode to Walter Allen)

Style, too, can abolish the boundaries between art and life. Simmons's theatre includes some memorable final acts in which the power of the completed performance mitigates pity and terror, for instance when the expertise of the 'Dead Birdman' at last lets him down:

Dumping backstage
his own, his human clothes,
he jumped, and seemed a wonder of the age.

But there is a didactic as well as a dramatic element in Simmons's poetry. One part of his imagination desires to change the world, not simply to stage it as it is. When he founded the literary magazine, *The Honest Ulsterman*, in 1968, he called it 'a monthly handbook for a revolution'. With varying degrees of self-mockery, he adopts the persona of a 'teacher', a 'reformer', in several poems:

and still I labour to build a country fit
for heroes, knowing you'd want no part of it.
(A Reformer to his Father)

This is where the immediacy of Simmons's poetry shades into urgency, as the manager of 'A crappy bookshop in a country town' discovers to his cost:

'Shame on you, sir,' I whisper in his ear.
'Such language, when a young person can hear.'
'It's true. It's urgent. What else could I say?'

'That's how the poet feels,' I smile. 'Good day.'
(Censorship)

'Urgency' and 'truth' also come together in the dialogue, 'For'/'Against', which could be the older Simmons arguing with his younger self. In 'For' the speaker advising his 'far-out/nephew' to 'take the long view' realises that the result will be to make the nephew 'as rotten/as you are, his urgent truths forgotten'. 'Against' displays the virtues of compromise in a better light:

And you won't – you won't want to – change the
  nation
because you'll know how little you understand.
The best – the good best – is a variation
on a popular tune. A new heaven *and*
a new earth is either a daily event or not to be.
I am not Jesus Christ, and neither was he.

Nevertheless, and despite that final disclaimer, Simmons's poetry has continued to propagate what might be called a libertarian philosophy. When attacking literary targets he consistently sends up 'the po-face/of court and bourgeois modes'. Correspondingly, in his broader criticism of the status quo, he figures as an outsider, an iconoclast, an egalitarian; sides with allegedly hollow men, the failures in life's organised competitions, anyone not mortgaged to an orthodoxy who is capable of finding 'Something that no one taught us to expect'. Most strikingly of all, he takes the part of Stephano, Trinculo and Caliban against their 'masters':

  a drunk butler's slower with a knife
than your fine courtiers, your dukes, your kings.
We were distracted by too many things . . .
the wine, the jokes, the music, fancy gowns.
We were no good as murderers, we were clowns.
(Stephano Remembers)

Simmons's more positive ideology inverts the version of puritanism still formidable in Northern Ireland by insisting that making love is better than making war or your peace with God. In its visionary aspect, his poetry is that of a Blakean Utopian who, somewhere beyond irony and qualification, believes with Judy Garland in somewhere over the rainbow, in the millennium he outlines in 'For Thomas Moore':

> when youth finds its singers
> and old men find peace
> and beauty finds servants
> and genius release . . .

Songwriters, singers and musicians are often given a prophetic role that reflects Simmons's wish to see his own 'songs' used 'to live and die with'. The original jazz revolution points the way towards a society free of oppression and repression, founded on and cherishing the unaggressive values of art, true to the spiritual implications of 'the word of life':

> Here was the risen people, their feet
> dancing, not out to murder the elite . . .
> *(Didn't He Ramble)*

Yet another deftly turned couplet emphasises the shapely clarity of Simmons's style, a clarity which is integral to the democracy of his approach. Songs and ballads of course aim at instant penetration of the mind and emotions, and it is likely that the discipline of these modes has toned up the muscle of Simmons's other verse, helping him to achieve surprisingly often his ideal of 'Tough reasonableness and lyric grace/ together'. The Elizabethan simplicity of phrasing in 'The Silent Marriage' and 'The Blessed Mary Hegarty', the streamlined economy of such different narratives as 'Summer Lightning' on the one hand, 'The Ballad of Gerry Kelly: Newsagent' and 'Claudy' on the other, have their echoes and equivalents throughout his work. In some ways the basis – or at least the base – of Simmons's poetry is statement, the medium of 'Tough reasonableness'. Despite an abundance of precise detail and vivid impressions, sensual impact generally plays second mate to the moralist or seer at the helm. Their idiomatic and dramatic energy rescue Simmons's statements from the pitfalls of abstraction, but his eagerness to place, as well as evoke, experience makes the epigrammatic couplet, the sonnet, the neat quatrain, forms to which he homes a trifle automatically. He is similarly adept at pacing a parable ('Lot's Wife', 'Flight'), or carving an emblem:

For every year of life we light
a candle on your cake
to mark the simple sort of progress
anyone can make,
and then, to test your nerve or give
a proper view of death,
you're asked to blow each light, each year
out with your own breath.

The mimetic quality of this 'Birthday Poem', however, proves Simmons's ability to break free of the rhythmic straitjacket (and fixed viewpoint) which his addiction to firmly rhymed iambic assertion sometimes becomes.

All my quotations illustrate the richness of diction, imagery and texture that can flesh out the poetry's strong bones. Myth supplies a further dimension still: in addition to the *Odyssey* and *King Lear* many subsidiary legends, folk tales, works of literature, as well as the poet's own inventiveness, open out, heighten and universalise a vision that occasionally risks becoming too particular or personal.

'Stephano Remembers' seems to me Simmons's most profound interpretation of an archetype; perhaps because dramatic and mythic qualities fuse at a whiter heat than usual, the imagery achieves a bolder 'sweep':

on a huge hogshead of claret I swept ashore
like an evangelist aboard his god . . .

But the fundamental source of the poem's excellence must be its extra distillation of the warmth and compassion which are the controlling emotions of Simmons's best work. They not only blossom forth in his love poems and his poems about children, but also determine a celebratory bias ('celebrate' is a favourite word). Truth to life, a realistic theatre, inevitably involves the poet in the seamier and darker side of existence, in violent 'Experience'; yet he can transfigure the blemishes that flesh is heir to:

a present of life,
bald head and flattened ears,
parcelled in blood and slime,
a loosely wrapped thing,
unlabelled but on time,
string dangling.
(Join Me in Celebrating)

It may be harder for Northern poets these days to 'join in celebrating' or come up with affirmations of life. Certainly 'Claudy' and 'The Ballad of Gerry Kelly' magnificently meet the new demands that have been made on compassion:

Sorting out the evening papers
while his son is selling sweets,
in our time, our town, two gunmen
walk in off the streets.

The last couplet of 'In Memoriam: Judy Garland' signals the ultimately curative spirit of James Simmons's achievement:

Discs are turning. Needles touch the rings
of dark rainbows. Judy Garland sings.

* * *

The above (with slight differences) appeared as a preface to *The Selected James Simmons*, published in 1978 by The Blackstaff Press. *Poems 1956-1986* includes a number of poems omitted from that selection, poems from *Constantly Singing* (1980) and *From the Irish* (1985), and some more recent work hitherto uncollected. In *Constantly Singing* Simmons's saga of the emotions takes a new turn: divorce and re-marriage, mid-life crisis. This focus deepens his perennial concern with the profit and loss of changing relationships as time moves on:

Twenty years is a long time to play
at marriage; but all my gardens
went to seed, all our houses
decayed in my tenancy.

Overall, Simmons's various 'meditations in time of divorce' blend into a bitter-sweet unity the moods of guilty valediction and joyous epithalamium:

The years from war to war
must be worth living for.

I sing of natural forces,
marriages, divorces.

(*Cloncha*)

In both *Constantly Singing* and *From the Irish* Simmons continues to harness the natural forces of ballad and song. But *From the Irish* also draws on traditional models in a new way by translating the spirit, if not the letter, of some Gaelic originals. Thus 'The Old Woman of Portrush' and 'Lament for a Dead Policeman' rework 'The Old Woman of Beare' and 'The Lament for Art O'Leary'. 'Lament for a Dead Policeman' incorporates a more political viewpoint than do Simmons's earlier elegies. Although neutral in juxtaposing the perspectives of the policeman's Protestant widow and his Catholic sister, who thinks him a deluded traitor to the tribe, the poem implicitly questions or broadens Irish martyrology by proclaiming an RUC man as worthy of lamentation as O'Leary. The title-poem of *From the Irish* demythologises by more concentrated means:

> Familiar things, you might brush against or tread
> upon in the daily round, were glistening red
> with the slaughter the hero caused, though he had gone.
> By proxy his bomb exploded, his valour shone.

Terence Brown has commented* on the 'topographical imperative' whereby 'poets of Protestant background' state their claim to an Irish identity by establishing associations with place. He quotes Simmons's 'Cloncha':

> The Anglo-Irish boy adores
> broken demesne walls,
> empty condemned cottages,
> moorlands littered with boulders
> gold-braided thinly with lichen . . .

However, he goes on to show how, far from being disabled by any *angst* of historical obsolescence, Simmons has repopulated a poetic landscape in vigorously contemporary terms. As well as transforming 'Anglo-Irish' idioms with reference to the different experience of a (renegade) Ulster Protestant, Simmons also transforms the religious idioms of his own tribe. Evangelism has always tinged the didactic aspect of the poetry. As for the visionary aspect, in 'The Farther Shore' an old

*in *Across a Roaring Hill*, ed. G. Dawe and E. Longley (Blackstaff Press, 1985)

woman broods on 'an old phrase from the hymnal'. The poem ends by identifying heaven with the warmly human:

The farther shore
is a real place where we spent our holidays.

It might be said that in various senses Simmons's poetry redeems those potentially bleak north-coast seasides on which it is founded.

Edna Longley

What these folk needed then was a reign of terror and a guillotine, and I was the wrong man for them.

Mark Twain, *A Connecticut Yankee at King Arthur's Court*

Ballad of a Marriage

'This sweet, mysterious country
explored by my right hand.
Am I the first, my wife, that's burst
into this silent land?'
She said she hadn't been a whore,
but she had lain with men before.

I'd slept with girls myself, but I
was trembling, I was hating
these men, and her, and yet I found
her stories titillating:
first fascination, then disgust;
first pain, and then a surge of lust.

Playing with words as children play
with toys had been a thrill,
but now the cuddly lion had jaws,
the little gun could kill.
Freedom and Truth, by which I swear,
in fact were more than I could bear.

When she stirred under me I saw her
squirming in delight
in other people's cars and beds,
and sitting up all night,
her face drained white in love's despair
because some man had not been there.

To freeze the pain of this I froze
my love. I read much more
and thought alone and talked to friends
till 3 a.m. and 4.
And came to bed the worse for beer,
and was annoyed to have her near.

She cried a lot and fought, surprised;
knowing love she felt the lack.
Love? What was love? I only felt
her dead weight on my back.
We stayed together out of shame
and habit, and then children came.

But books and thought and talk aren't drugs,
they query and accuse:
where do you hope to go from here?
What are you going to lose?
And just to fight and tell her lies
I had to look and see her eyes.

As green shoots push through hardened soil
where nothing seemed to be,
so tenderness, caresses, jokes
grew out of her and me.
No families wave, no organs play,
this long and gradual wedding day.

The Not Yet Ancient Mariner

Before he settled to his hard vocation
he must just taste the youth that others had,
be ordinary. He put dark glasses on
and sauntered smiling down the promenade.

There it was usual to chat with strangers.
At first he was quite affable and pliant
until some point involved him, his eyes glittered,
'There was this ship,' he said, blushing, defiant.

Words were too precious to be easy with him –
the painful urgency to get things right.
Most girls he cornered, bored by protestations
so qualified, chalked up a wasted night.

He managed to make nicer girls unhappy,
some guilty, some uncertain, some just small,
made little hands applying lipstick tremble
before they left for church or dancing hall.

His solitude, he saw, was part of greatness:
what cut him off was all the things they'd missed;
but when he said goodnight to casual strangers
why did his face still bend down to be kissed?

Puzzled or shocked, some turned their cheeks away.
What was the kiss about? He didn't know.
Some, casual or curious, kissed him back;
but any time was time for him to go.

Here was no solace and no recreation.
There was, as he'd suspected from the start,
no place within his chosen life that chose him
for trivialities so near his heart.

To a Dead Birdman

All explanation is a lie.
I watched this birdman falling,
a little figure in the sky
neither dancing nor calling.

Sooner or later some flaw
in his contraptions or his skill
would let him down. This we foresaw.
Waiting was part of the thrill.

As brave as Christ? Drawn near
three times a day to death
for a few thousand a year
and people's held breath?

Showy, but no fake,
it was death he risked. He died
precisely at the first mistake,
and had a right to pride

if that was it. Why sacrifice
where no one stands to gain?
In free fall from the skies
he conquered pain,

perhaps; but courage is like treasure,
calling for proper use.
Breaking a vessel only to measure
its strength is abuse.

So, what did he betray?
What made him draw
our eyes away
from what we didn't see to what we saw?

He wins, for no one knows.
Dumping backstage
his own, his human clothes,
he jumped, and seemed a wonder of the age.

Lust

Drunk stranger, manoeuvering me
laughing towards the bed,
more or less indifferent
to what I have just said,
I shrug you off in anger
and walk quickly away
to be alone in the bathroom:
it is as bright as day.
That sudden darkening of the mind
doesn't survive here.
Among the shining taps and tiles
I smile at my fear.
Your glimpsed, crestfallen face revives
happily in my mind.
Is this not what I wanted,
what I had hoped to find
after the dance was over,
after walking home with you?
I don't remember what I said
that you weren't listening to.
Lust stirs in me as well. I can't
tell lust and love apart,
nor does it seem to matter. Please
go easy past my heart.

The Archæologist

Portrush. Walking dead streets in the dark.
Winter. A cold wind off the Atlantic
rattling metal in the amusement park.

Rain. The ornate dancehall, empty on the rocks,
bright paint worn thin, posters half torn away,
sweet-stalls, boarded up and locked with padlocks.

Returned to the scene, at once I see again
myself, when ten years younger, and a girl,
preserved in an almost perfect state by the brain.

That is her window, high on the side wall.
Beneath it figures, projected by the mind,
are moving. I am about to call.

I give her name and wait. She is called down.
Without taking thought I know what I want to do.
Love, like electric current, lights the town.

Nothing is tawdry, all our jokes are funny,
the pin-table is brighter than Shakespeare's works,
my handful of warm coins is sufficient money.

Imaginative reconstruction shed
some light upon a vanished way of life.
I cannot live like them, and they are dead.

The cold makes me simpler and breaks the spell:
I don't mind crying, but I hate to shiver,
and walk quickly back to my hotel.

Sonnet for the Class of '58

No longer students and not likely to succeed,
tonight I remember old friends, scattered far,
who wanted so much once, and now need
only a rise of a hundred pounds or a car
or a holiday abroad without the wife,
or time to read more, or more fun.
Perhaps never, or only when drunk, does life
seem as it once seemed, a war to be won.
The moving and influential things they devised
have all been said and done, it seems, by others.
Some do the very things that they despised
and recognise the enemy as brothers;
and even those who've gained more power or sense
feel sorry when they feel the difference.

Roots

He left the circus, settled in Coleraine,
wild, stylish, garrulous, uneducated
and met this lovely Presbyterian
whose face he worshipped, and whose views he hated,
her body in drab clothes, her lips pursed tight,
up from Fermanagh to be someone's maid;
he made her mad with joy – that wasn't right! –
but one cramped smile said all that need be said.

Her soul was lost, though marriage saved her honour.
The child was sly and pretty; she could see
its waywardness must be a judgement on her:
their love was wanton, and their child would be.
She was: she brought *me* home. Christ, what a row!
'That bearded freak!' I heard the mother cry.

We married, though, and live in Queensland now,
as free as if we'd dropped out of the sky.

Me and the World

I live with photographs
for the world, my girl, is away mostly,
estranged by flaws of mine or withdrawn
for her own reasons. She will always surprise me,
and some days when I open my eyes
she is present to every sense.
It makes all the difference.
My hands answer faster than blind men
at braille, learn by the lover's touch
what news I need in all her double Dutch:
and ears and eyes are distinct and expert by sorrow
knowing she is here today and gone tomorrow.

Fidgeting birdsong, the tram's lurch and slide
are henceforward my girl's perfect nonsense.
Together we walk, in the bar she sits at my side.
Her pencil stump worn down with words,
my left hand resting face down on her table,
her amber pint of beer, tobacco shreds,
this atmosphere of this, her morning,
are on speaking terms with my head.
Outside the crippled houses respond
to the continual miracle of sun and dust.
Roofs, railings and the time of year
walk beautifully together because they must.
And rare colours, blended by hard wear,
on cheap cottons of city children
invite, not pity, but the satisfaction of love.
The rare ointment of formal praise
is suddenly useful on such wedding days.
I serve and sway the land. Standing
more like a child than lover, I hold her hand
and listen. Missing perhaps the point of the story,
grateful, stupid, smiling, I share the glory.

My smile is genuine, though when she laughs
I don't forget my jar to warm the bed, my photographs.

Ode to Blenheim Square

for George Campbell

Declining houses, still tall,
on two sides of the square,
on two sides a crumbling wall,
enclose a garden, worn bare
of grass in bald patches, defaced
by rubbish. The railings and gate,
removed for the last war, were not replaced,
and now it is too late;
the people that this square was built to please
have long since gone,
and artists, students, refugees,
once admitted, cling on.

Even the trees are dirty to touch,
the undug clay, hard:
a bit of Nature, but not much
better than a concrete yard.
You can't lie down for dog-shit.
But every morning, lovely, lonely,
through white mist, lit
by the hidden sun, only
greenness and brightness show,
and, sharp against the sky, aloof,
as your eyes reach from below,
the everywhere elegant lines of branch and roof.
The blemishes don't show
at sunset either,
or under snow.
That beauty is hidden is in its favour;
I don't give garden parties.

I am content
to have no better times than these,
and no other environment.

Last Sunday I came
downstairs and saw the door, ajar,
and grimed fanlight frame
the garden
while I stood inside,
the Dutch painters' view in reverse,
also in my house-pride
being perverse.
But a cheap rent on what I love
is guaranteed by decay:
rich and poor disapprove
in the same way.

Husband to Wife

When I consider how your life was spent
before we met, I see a parked car
where some man took you, dear, with your consent,
and helped to make you what you are.
From both of you there is the smell of beer;
I feel you thrilled at last to be alone,
not missing me – well, how could I be there! –
exploring him and being explored and known.
My fancy pushes towards pornography
the necessary sweet acts of lust.
Then you undid his flies, unblushingly,
with cool hands, then a joke, a smile of trust,
then took his weight and smelt and felt his breath,
then held and guided underneath your skin
his rosy, swelling penis, in a sheath,
filling you up as it came in,
just as mine does, my bride,
just as mine does. Such thoughts have made me sweat
and wrestle hours, no, years, against my pride;
and, to be honest, I am wrestling yet.
You are because you were, and when I love
I love because and not in spite of this,
and you, not waiting till I rise above,
cleave to uneasiness.

Macushla, Machree

She is scarred like a soldier,
she droops like a jelly,
there are three distinct ridges
of fat on her belly.
There are varicose veins
on her legs, at the back.
Her vagina is more
a crevasse than a crack.

But I love the old ruin;
each defect and flaw
commemorates something
that both of us saw.
Be it car-crash or childbirth,
each line tells a story,
has a moral, my love,
my *memento mori*.

Lot's Wife

Uneasiness confirmed his words were right:
there was a rottenness in all she knew.
She could not see where she was going to
but love for him felt stronger than her fright.

Yet as she travelled on she was bereft
of every landmark but her husband's eyes:
her whole life echoed in her friends' goodbyes.
How could he take the place of all she left?

For him or them, but not for heaven's sake,
she made decisions: these two were opposed.
He led her on his way, her eyes were closed.
At every step she felt her heart would break.

At last Lot drew his wagon to a halt;
dog-tired but glad, he groped his way inside,
looking for pleasure in his sleeping bride,
kissed her, and on her cold cheek tasted salt.

For John Clare

Lucky John, your lady, hard to get,
lived in the grave. Lucky John walking
hard miles (in your mad mood, easy)
all hedge and thistle homewards, nowhere.
Imagination decorates flat marshes
you grew (in a way) up in, all with Mary
till keepers, John, kindly enough, return you,
keeping your feet on, but above, the ground.

And Pedro too, the Runswick idiot, sketching
himself with princess can hold us and her,
and walks, as long as visitors will listen,
the streets of Monte Carlo, long familiar
from nightly lingering in a book with pictures;
for he turns pages as people shake hands,
and that is a great talent.
                                        Pedro, John,
bless the girls that I lie on, for I
who loved Illona Massey at fourteen
with a great love am now a has-been.

Written, Directed by and Starring . . .

The scripts I used to write for the young actor –
me – weren't used. And now I couldn't play
the original parts and, as director,
I'd turn myself, if I applied, away.

My break will come; but now the star's mature
his parts need character and 'love' is out.
He learns to smile on birth and death, to endure:
it's strange I keep the old scripts lying about.

Looking them over I've at times forgot
they've never been put on. I seem to spend
too much time reading through a final shot
where massed choirs sing, they kiss, and then THE END.

It's hard to start upon this middle phase
when my first period never reached the screen,
and there's no end now to my new screen-plays,
they just go on from scene to scene to scene.

The hero never hogs the screen because
his wife, his children, friends, events intrude.
When he's not on the story doesn't pause –
not if he dies. I don't see why it should.

Experience

‘I want to fight you,’ he said in a Belfast accent.
Amazed and scared, with hurried words I resisted.
‘Fighting solves nothing. Tell me how I’ve annoyed you,’
I said. But more insulted the man persisted.

In the lavatory he squared his fists and approached me:
‘Now you can talk.’ I backed over cold stone in
a room that contained us and joined us. ‘It’s all so silly,’
I pleaded, searching for spaces to be alone in.

I shrank from his strangeness, not only afraid.
But at last of course I suffered what could not be delayed,
the innocuous struggle, the fighting words, ‘bastard’ and ‘fuck’,
a torn shirt and my lip numb and bloody,
my anger and – strange – the feel of my own body
new to me, as I struck, as he struck.

To a Cigarette

Friend Judas, kiss me,
stain my fingers brown,
start a malignant growth;
I'll burn you down.
Friends for fifteen years
and I doubt whether
a week has passed
without us being together.

My mouth's foul in the morning,
but you stay in favour
although you've spoilt my sense of smell
and food's losing its flavour.
You're still and all my good friend,
your faint odour thrills me.
It seems I'm always going to love you
even if it kills me.

Friends are often dangerous
even when they're kind.
Girls with skin as fresh as cream
have left disease behind,
and drink, that's made so many nights
so memorably funny,
perforates my liver, drains
my energy and money.

I am in peril on the sea,
I roll my eyes and yelp;
but feel no hatred or surprise
for those too scared to help.
I dream of love, I am hungry;
but I'll accept in the end,
with no diminishing of love,
your empty hands, friend.

A Reformer to his Father

We shared not one idea in thirty years
of occasional bicker and chat. One night of loud
useless argument, unique and useless tears
of mine surprised us. We paused, astute and proud,
unreconciled. I think I had stopped hearing
your words, and heard around me the rest,
unknown, remote, and thought I was comparing
the sound of your worst with their best.
Subservient to love I bent my head
stiffly. You laughed, nervous, elated, and laid
nicotined fingers lightly on and said
nothing. Never again, and now you are dead;
and still I labour to build a country fit
for heroes, knowing you'd want no part of it.

Lullaby for Rachael

All your days are holy days,
in dreams begins your terror.
Predetermined are the ways
perfection comes to error.

Flaws, like hands used in the sun,
will gradually harden.
You, as your elders did, will run
from simple things, from the garden.

Sleeping when each day is through
practise for your death.
Learn each law you're subject to
within your lease of breath.

My world is mapped imperfectly:
here I once found treasure,
friends here, here the enemy;
alter it with pleasure.

Changing the boundary lines, I fear,
has made my map a mess.
By seeing more you may draw clear,
but not by seeing less.

The lullaby was adequate,
you'll sleep until the morning.
How little we communicate,
how useless is this warning.

Though I have failed to make you wise
with all the words above,
I've made, while trying to tell no lies,
a noise to go with love.

A Muse

The one I use
is not a moral Muse.
When I'm inadequate
or spite twists me or hate,
or I'm fresh from half-baked sin,
she still comes smiling in
before I'm sorry (and I never ask)
with a full hip-flask
and cigarettes. What's more,
she reclines on the floor,
naked, without a word.

I seldom fail to be stirred
to our mutual satisfaction
and charmed by her kind action.

She walks out into the street;
but our child is my receipt,
a dutiful offspring, glad
to earn cash for his old dad.
It is quite true his mother hates
men who would make dates,
and leaves them hanging about.
There is even some doubt
if fidelity excites her,
however fervent and bright. Her
charm is in being chancy.
She comes at her own fancy
to delight her host
at the weirdest and most
memorable hours.
                    The features
of this delightful creature
are sometimes seen

on others' children. She has been,
to annoy me, elsewhere with her passion,
behaving, doubtless, in the above fashion.

Ballad of New Frontiers

When Boston grew too much like home
we left the coast behind us
and inland then began to roam
where people wouldn't mind us.
We lifted old guns down from shelves
and fought for space to be ourselves.

No one prevented us, we rode
across the savage land.
Those who survived cleared ground and sowed
with friends and guns at hand.
We cherished one another well
until we learnt to buy and sell.

The boundaries grew, the laws increased,
the camp became a town.
The brotherhood and hardship ceased
and rules got written down.
The old constraints brought discontent
and so we sold our claims and went.

Our battered rifles oiled again,
we set the wagons rolling
westward. We found, in grassy plains,
the emptiness consoling.
The chance was still there to achieve
homes we would never want to leave.

We staggered down the mountainside
and stood on that great shore,
thankful the waters seemed too wide
for us to travel more;
knowing what our fathers did not know –
they'd fled in vain long years ago.

‘We can’t escape,’ Max cried in fun,
‘our cell’s this coastal plain,
our prison warden is the sun –
come on, someone, complain!
The common sentence is Hard Labour
here as elsewhere. Start digging, neighbour!’

George Campbell started back alone,
his son went up the coast.
Some settled down reluctantly.
Joe Carr we pitied most;
Joe took his gun – too old, too tired –
and stuck it in his mouth and fired.

But one man shouted, ‘This is where
I’ve always longed to be,
with fertile ground and salty air,
hills at the back of me.
Out of the desert of the past
thank God I’ve stumbled here at last.’

The Smiths and Butlers sang a hymn.
The boss made out a list
of basic duties. Joan and Jim,
beneath a wagon, kissed,
grown more adept in copulation
at every stop across the nation.

Madge Thompson lifted down her pans
and cut up meat for stew.
Her husband saw it was a chance
to contemplate the view
and urinate among the rocks
and check the progress of his pox.

Few wished to sing – we weren't being fooled –
and as the night got colder
we lay, the old rough blankets pulled
up round familiar shoulders,
aware of sounds we'd heard before
off Boston on the Eastern shore.

In the Wilderness

I sit alone on the rocks trying to prepare
a man to teach what the laws of life are.
Sunlight and silence, nurses against disease,
are busy fighting my infirmities.
The life is simple, you could not say rough,
a stream, some cans and firewood are enough
to live on; but a hostile shift of weather
would bring me sharply up on the short tether
of endurance. We haven't survived by strength alone.
We have neither fur nor fangs. I will go home,
just as I rise from sleep, eat and get dressed.
This is one more resort, not last or best.

A teacher in the wilderness alone
learns to make bread and sermons out of stone.

The Influence of Natural Objects

for Bill Ireland

Night after night from our camp on Sugar Loaf Hill
we strolled the streets, roaring or quiet, daring
anything for girls or drink, but not caring
when the town closed. We reeled home and were ill,
cooked fries, fell senseless in our socks
on grass or blankets. I woke cold at dawn
and stumbled to the Hill Top Zoo, and on
through pines to the bare summit's litter of rocks.
I was always scared by the huge spaces below,

between sky and water, explosive bright air
glinting on live-wire nerves of mine, worn bare.
I lay down, grinning, stiff with vertigo.

This roused an appetite for breakfast, bars,
bathing, chasing the daft holiday bitches,
for jokes and poems, beer and sandwiches . . .
and so on till we slept under the stars.

Outward Bound

for Tony Harrison

Two campers (King Lear and his clown?)
smile to see the skies come down.
The shaken mind finds metaphors
in winds that shake the great outdoors.
As roofs and fences fall in storms
the tranquil mind's protective forms
collapse when passion, grief and fear
stir. We will spend a fortnight here.

To this small wilderness we bring
ourselves to play at suffering,
to swim in lonely bays, immerse
in the destructive elements, nurse
our bare forked bodies by wood fires
where ox-tail soup in mugs inspires
the tender flesh. By rocks we cough
and shiver in the wind, throw off
what history has lent, and lie
naked, alone, under the sky.

Of course, not one of us prefers
the cold; we are sun-worshippers,
wilderness- and storm-defiers,
neither masochists nor liars.

Cheeks whipped by freezing rain go numb.
The baffled blood is stirred, will come
again, glowing like my mind when Lear
speaks in the words of Shakespeare.
Under duress trying to sing
in tune, foretasting suffering
that we will swallow whole, the storm

endured, we hope to come to harm
at home, with better dignity
or style or courage. Anyway
I like to camp and read *King Lear*.
We had a lovely fortnight here.

At Cordelia's Grave

France speaks

1.
My wife: a martyr.
I have undressed her
small, perfect body
which is holy now,
caressed her white throat,
bruised where the rope
choked her. She liked to joke
about my reasonableness.
She would undress
quite unselfconsciously,
pursuing a theory,
(all mind and voice and eyes,
she thought) and be surprised
when my arms bound her,
and angrily protest,
shaking herself, detaching
me from her breasts,
wild that I'd missed the point
of her disjointed argument.

2.
The acuteness of her love
had made her silent, not pride.
Her love and her dear father would be justified
when time taught him to see the only way.
I could agree; but then, 'My father is being tried
too far – and tried by whom?' she'd say.
'None of these people understands his ways
like me. There isn't time for holidays!'
'Not holidays,' I said. 'Your life is here.

He must choose now, you've made the issues clear.
This follows from your silence. You weren't cold
but wise, kind in the bravest way.' She said, 'He's old.'

3.
I gave her many good and interesting gifts,
new friends with wit and courage equal to hers.
While they were analysing and construing
and recommending liberal reforms, she'd say,
'I must go home. Find out what Goneril's doing.
If power is necessary, I should have lied.
Truth is a luxury and I'd rather
stop serving ideals and serve my father.'
I told her there was no controlling outcomes:
'Your father would have suffered either way.
Pain is the rent on life. Whoever chooses
wisely will still suffer when others lose.'
'Well, then, I should have stayed, like Kent.'
My patience tried too far, I said,
'Kent has the virtues of an English dog, that's all.
He serves blindly, barks at his master's enemies,
comes to his call, always, and finally dies
on his master's grave . . . humorous, brave, useful;
but for all his good service, what will he save?'
She only answered, 'He's better than you or I.
Give me your army.' And I, to please her,
have let my own countrymen go to die.
Why are so many involved? Why? Why?

4.
Oh, they were fascinators – Lear and his children –
mad, bad, treacherous. All of them found

faithful servants to watch and set forward
their family spree of love and hate. They cared
nothing for us, all for their damned family,
and yet I am crying, I am ready to lie down
and die like Gloucester did and Kent will, like the clown.

5.
She would have loved explaining why
she had left me, and had to die;
but I will never hear, alas,
her sweet analysis
again. She never counted on
the future that I counted on
I thought she was so glad
to be rescued from her mad
father and sisters.
                                        I try
to see all this objectively:
she lost the war,
her father, herself, me.
Albany and Gloucester's son
fill up the vacant places.
That comment would have bored
her. But what was won?
They say she was restored
to the good graces
of her father, and they ignored
their gaolers, made fun
that little while in prison,
remembering when she was young,
they say, they say, they say,
morose, self-satisfied,
and no one looks my way.

A Speech for the Clown

Not just my patter, my mind's oblique,
but I spoke on when you refused to speak.
Old wise men worship you, but I'd rather
you'd played up to your daft old father.
True? To a moral law's dead letter?
Something less abstract would have served better.
They were violent people always, but some yoke
controlled them that your silence broke.

When luck chose that same hour to bring
your recognition by the French king,
my spite and sorrow saw a lack
of tact in such quick joy; but back
you came at last and suffered too,
and knelt to him. He knelt to you,
for he was wiser when he died,
so maybe you were justified.

Soon on your birthdays churchbells will be rung,
for power went to the faithful and the young
when Albany and Edgar shared the crown;
but I'm no longer fitted for a clown.
Mad as my dead master, no reform
can change what changed me during the storm.

For Ruth Ellis

executed 1955

The contract love insists on has a clause
admitting disappointment as just cause
for killing. Don Juan accepts danger
as an occupational risk, without anger.
If words won't do and there's no place to run,
unfaithful lovers ought to face the gun.

This good tradition can be undermined
by those who shoot before the contract's signed
and find disgust or horror in dying eyes,
not just exasperation or surprise.
To kill well needs some talent, as to kiss:
the inept or nasty will still be so in this.

The newspapers are quite right to report
this act as they do carnivals or sport.
A man is dead, but jealous girls don't chill
the blood; soldiers and hangmen do who kill
strangers on strangers' orders, their paid work
to stick with a bayonet, make a rope jerk.

Join Me in Celebrating

Join me in celebrating
this unhoped-for gift
she has brought me sweating
in a crumpled shift.
Pushed through my wife,
my letterbox, appears
a present of life,
bald head and flattened ears,
parcelled in blood and slime,
a loosely wrapped thing,
unlabelled but on time,
string dangling.
I wouldn't change my condition
for freedom, cash, applause,
rebirth of young ambition
or faith in Santa Claus.

Art and Reality

for James Boyce

From twenty yards I saw my old love
locking up her car.
She smiled and waved, as lovely still
as girls of twenty are –

that cloud of auburn hair that bursts
like sunrise round her head,
the smile that made me smile
at ordinary things she said.

But twenty years have gone and flesh
is perishable stuff;
can art and exercise and diet
ever be enough

to save the tiny facial muscles
and keep taut the skin
and have the waist, in middle-age,
still curving firmly in?

Beauty invites me to approach
and lies make truth seem hard
as my old love assumes her age,
a year for every yard.

The Prodigal Thinks of his Mother

Five o'clock in February,
full moon in a cold grey sky.
Mother, if you saw me now
I know that you would cry.

It makes me nervous in my joy
to think what you would see
in this flat and this sleeping girl
who, last night, slept with me.

Yet surely you remember
(for both our sakes you must)
the tenderness of passion,
the innocence of lust?

I know she isn't new to love –
you'd make a lot of that,
but I don't think of it: she likes
her comfort like a cat.

My love, how could I leave her?
The way she turns her head
so self-absorbed, I smile and make
a pot of tea instead.

Black branches at the window
sink ink-stains in the sky,
reminding me of how your face
would turn to me and cry,

crumpled with disappointment,
murmuring through tears,
'Is this the end of the great hopes
we had of you for years?'

And I can't make you promises,
for soon the girl will wake,
and when she smiles I will not frown
for anybody's sake.

You have no time for arguments,
there is no way to prove
that what we do is decent, dear,
not lewdness if not love,

sin is too big a word, our bodies'
thrills, our hearts' small aches
should trouble nobody. We laugh,
not weep at our mistakes.

Five o'clock in February,
full moon in a quiet sky:
because you are my mother
this scene would make you cry.

Because you are what you are
you must withdraw your hand
from blessing. Sometimes I'm angry,
sometimes I understand.

Letter to a Jealous Friend

You could not say, 'What now?' You said, 'Too late!'
What energies bad principles have spilt.
Old friend, you hate me and you aggravate
me, for I will not feel regret or guilt

when your white face stares at me from the door
with wizard eyes that change the three of us
into a cuckold, a roué, a whore –
a stupid, ugly metamorphosis.

Acquaintances are mocking my belief
that we could still be friends when it was known.
I tremble when you treat me like a thief;
but I touched nothing you can call your own.

A child might own the doll it sleeps beside
and men own money and what money buys;
but no one earns a friend or owns his bride
however much he needs or hard he tries.

You try to run me over with your bus
and call me out of restaurants to fight.
I smile weakly and wait for all the fuss
to fade. I need to get my sleep at night.

I hear in some domestic tiff she tossed
our love at you and scored. Each time I try
to fit that in my creed I lose my place.
There's more in animals than meets the eye.

Sweet fun and freedom didn't last for long
with you out shouting we'd betrayed your trust.
We said it was our business. We were wrong.
Your jealousy's as natural as our lust.

Our thoughts of other people paralyse
our minds and make us act the silly parts
we think they cast us in. Feeling their eyes
on us, we seem to lose touch with our hearts.

Crippled by hate you have to crouch in dude
levis and dark glasses, glaring at us.
We have to lie unnaturally nude
and vulnerable, trapped, ridiculous.

In the Desert War

Of four friends three survive. One is dead drunk,
another walked in darkness by the sea
and now lies, stiff with sorrow, in his bunk.
We, in our minds, and wild dogs really,
drag out that corpse from the shallow grave we made.
Four friends foresaw such resurrections
before the battle and laughed and were afraid.
I laugh, remembering, going into actions
he enjoyed, like this, glad to be human,
glad of my drinker's sway, my smoker's cough
that well might wake the husband of this woman
who giggles at me with my trousers off.
All his effects were sent off to his mother
except this contraceptive which I don
in memory. I wish his ghost could hover
over me, smiling, with a good hard-on.

A Birthday Poem

for Rachael

For every year of life we light
a candle on your cake
to mark the simple sort of progress
anyone can make,
and then, to test your nerve or give
a proper view of death,
you're asked to blow each light, each year,
out with your own breath.

Old Gardener

I kneel down painfully and touch the dirty lace
of cabbage leaves, all crinkled like my face
and preying hands, twisted, but still able
to pluck out weeds between the vegetables
and give them space freely to suck and chew
the soil their muscular stalks stick through.

Fifty years I've filled boxes for market
for men to buy and eat, digest and defecate.
The roar of teeth clashing fills my inner
ear. The world is always at dinner.
I hear the jaws of caterpillars ravage
the thick leaves of the hungry cabbage.

Older, weaker, never to be fatter,
I am frightened of chewing, chewing, chewing. Matter
is eating matter, and I, who buy and sell
and nurture ravagers, am chewed as well,
living between Jehovah's jaws until
the garden is empty and his grinders are still.

Revelation

My love has thick ankles,
her hips are too fat.
I never expected
I'd put up with that.

In theory I knew
but in practice demurred,
there is often more fun
with the dowdier bird.

Out here in the tropics
we're easier pleased
since whores got expensive
and brusque and diseased.

My bachelor's Taunus,
grey leather and chrome,
drives up for young women
I'd call plain at home.

I have worked at my tan
and my clothes-sense and brogue
so my women and I'd
look like pictures in *Vogue*.

But the girls who read *Vogue*
and are bored by Ted Hughes
are easy to look at
but hard to amuse.

Today, wide shorts flapping
and shirt out of style,
my jokes make this heavy
young graduate smile.

We read or just sit
when there's nothing to say,
and we don't have to lean
on each other all day.

She looks up in welcome,
I look down and trace
intelligence, humour
and warmth in her face,

where once I could only see
fuzzy, dry hair,
plain features, a poor skin,
a short-sighted stare.

Convenience became
revelation today.
'You are lovely. I love you,'
I heard myself say.

The End of the Affair

We could count the times we went for a walk
or the times we danced together in the past
months – if not the times of making love and talk.
Our first separation will be our last.

I suppose we never discussed what we have known:
that I am to go home, that you will stay.
All the mutual tenderness that has grown,
sweet as it is, is not to get in the way

of the work before us, mine and yours.
What has been given is being taken away,
and we aren't looking for loopholes and cures,
freely absenting ourselves from this felicity

to tell our story under plain covers
in bed, or by example, till everyone understands
that joy will not be bound. Artists and lovers
start and complete their work with empty hands.

To leave my wife and children for love's sake
and marry you would be a failure of nerve.
I remember love and all that goes to make
the marriage, the affairs, that I deserve.

I'll Never Say Goodbye

At the end of the Serpentine,
Lancaster Gate,
on a morning last January,
having to wait,
I walked where I used to walk
fifteen years gone
by the elegant, worn-away
fountains of stone.

Like a stone-shattered windscreen
the water rose white
against air on the left
and black trees on the right.
With small swans beside them,
in stone, at their ease,
were two big girls holding
their ewers on their knees.

Exactly your features,
the strength of your back,
the curve of your breasts
and the chin that you lack.
Your body a fountain
with life thrusting out,
and this must be the sister
you told me about.

This is my part of London.
I'm happy to know
that your statue looks down
where I once used to row,
and whenever I pass here
on poetry tours,
by the Serpentine fountains
my time will be yours.

One of the Boys

Our youth was gay but rough,
much drink and copulation.
If that seems not enough
blame our miseducation.
In shabby boarding houses
lips covered lips,
and in our wild carouses
there were companionships.
Cheap and mundane the setting
of all that we remember:
in August, dancehall petting,
cinemas in December.
Now middle-aged I know,
and do not hide the truth,
used or misused years go
and take all kinds of youth.
We test the foreign scene
or grow too fat in banks,
salesmen for margarine,
soldiers in tanks,
the great careers all tricks,
the fine arts all my arse,
business and politics
a cruel farce.
Though fear of getting fired
may ease, and work is hated
less, we are tired, tired
and incapacitated.
On golf courses, in bars,
crutched by the cash we earn,
we think of nights in cars
with energy to burn.

The Silent Marriage

A song

With your clothes on the chair
and one white sheet above you
I have no need of words
to explain how I love you.
Every touch of delight
through the long wedding night
is defining our love.
With this kiss I thee wed.

If our luck should run out
and love withers and dies, love,
don't try out of kindness
to save me with lies, love.
You won't need to explain
that I'm single again
and the marriage is done
when your kiss says goodbye.

Marital Sonnets

1.
She was brought up like most girls of that age
to rouse lust in the casual passerby.
Tight skirts and nylons and décolletage
stirred lust she wasn't taught to satisfy.
Her nerve and frankness made her seem a flirt
when all she really wanted was a friend.
Men talked until their hands were up her skirt:
she got it over, but it was the end.
Some, looking back, could sense that they had missed
something for which they hadn't been prepared.
They told their troubles to her and got pissed
and left. At twenty she was tired and scared,
bitter and frigid and without resource,
but still *the hottest thing in town*, of course.

2.
When I was twenty-four I was so lonely
I married her to keep me company
and learnt to value solitude the hard way.
It turned out that a husband must have money.
I fastened on the old chains I had broken,
I took direction and prepared to sit
exams, made notes on rubbish spoken
by cultivated hacks, was paid for it.
My joy in reading atrophied.
Hatred and guilt and laziness
increased. In drink I sneered or cried,
vomited up and ate my own mess,
and in due course had limited success
constructing poems from unhappiness.

3.
It seemed right to protect my poetry,
work in my study late at night, refuse
the household chores you wanted done, choose
these creative jobs, and not apply
for posts you read of with huge salaries,
enough to free you from constraint and worry
about the unpaid bills and worn clothes. I'm not sorry
you've missed out on the things your sister has.

Some nights you force the issue and we fight.
I threaten to walk out and sometimes do,
but there's the children, and alone at night
I wonder where I think I'm going to,
losing my kids and hurting them, for what?
Young women? Rave reviews? A Paris flat?

4.
We murmured passionate language in that trance
when each was famished for the mutual kiss;
but we have altered, and it spoils all chance
of happiness, comparing that with this.
Displays of fireworks were put on by lust,
romantic symphonies, unholy wars:
now contraceptives, unworn, gather dust,
in which we once soared gleaming towards the stars.
In age's Leamington our joys last longer,
the libraries are good, the tea-rooms neat,
good arguments aren't broken off by anger,
new appetites are fed, we are replete.
Let's call this love, that alters when it finds
alteration, the marriage of two minds.

5.

Night after night she rose when he rose, sat
in his room, apart, silently, able to lend him
some of her calm when the Muses seemed to rend him,
sketching and writing in that storm-torn flat.
She explained to strangers, 'Of Mr Blake's company
I have very little, he is always in Paradise.'
Lucky for Blake his wife set a high price
on a poet's thoughts. Mine might offer a penny.
She calls, 'You're always writing, you hardly see
your children.' Muttering, I come down to play,
discharging my duty, enjoying a sunny day,
deprived of guilt and opportunity.
But any Ulster man would blush to claim
his room deserved a more pretentious name.

6.

A man and wife lying, tired, side by side,
were bored and frightened, and they copulated
just to do something. Having done, they hated
each other. 'Things can't get worse,' he cried.
To prove him wrong she said that on that bed
Charley had laid her yesterday. Too late
to close her mouth when fear and hate
already had run wild inside his head.
They longed for boredom back, but the police
of consciousness, once called, won't drop a case.
They question, strip, detain, probe every place
till someone's brought to judgement. Then there's peace.
The pain of this can hardly be endured:
helplessly waiting to be killed or cured.

7.
I'll publish these. They aren't for you.
Writing is my ridiculous profession.
Husbands my age will maybe say how true
and tragic is my commonplace confession;
but ex-pupils, men born since the war,
holding their noses will despise the skill
and wonder what the stuff gets published for.
Why are their sordid elders at it still?

I helped create the free hygienic mind,
rid of the guilt and infantile self-hate
that we were subject to; but now I find
this world too kindly to the second-rate.
I miss the nervous, dirty-minded, sad,
clever, very funny friends I had.

Soliloquy for a Ghost

I am going home alone on Saturday
as a child goes back to Heaven – the longest way,
rattling every door to company.
They are all closed, even the library.
I walk familiar streets that are the scene
of my working life, my projects and routine,
from which each Friday, half past five, I flit
to home in Purgatory where I sit
in cold abstraction or go out to haunt
these streets; but I must wait for what I want.
A disappointed spirit with meal-time for a cock,
I start back as the bells say six o'clock
to the nicest woman I have ever met,
where my bed is made and tea-table set.

King Cophetua to the Beggar Maid

I was a king on a throne.
I wore embroidered robes
elegantly and alone.

I moved like the sun
through a full garden
bowing to everyone;

but love was rife,
to you I condescended
and shared my life.

You didn't understand
what a place you took
when I took your hand.

With common pluck and guile,
misunderstanding mine,
you stuck to your own style

and, more, prevented me
from being my lonely self.
Do you like what you see?

My throne looks like a chair,
my clothes vaguely pretentious,
my great room is bare
and my kingdom is not anywhere.

Protestant Courts Catholic

Too tired, and too fastidious for lies,
he said, 'Let's make love when you're free.'
'Just like that?' 'Yes, just like that. No ties.'
She said, 'You wouldn't want to marry me.'

Although his devious honesty made him sick,
'You'll give yourself to someone. Who?' he said.
'The unknown husband. I'm a Catholic,'
she smiled. He said, 'Don't smile and shake your head.'

Intrigued, he argued, but she never budged.
She blamed the church. He said she was a sham.
'You have to judge in order to be judged.'
Her smile was roguish, false. 'That's how I am.'

'Look, I'm the serpent you have read about.
The law says no, I'd like it if you would.
You're free either to stretch your fingers out
or not. Choose, knowledge or servitude.'

Seducer turned to saviour on a whim,
he lavished hours of rhetoric on her.
Her faith protected her from men like him,
useless at home, dynamic in a bar.

To be the star, attended, made her tremble.
How seriously drunken poets play;
but Irish girls are brought up to dissemble,
to blush and listen and to get their way.

'In these cases we still have judgement here.
It's you who'll suffer, so it can't be right
to leave choice to the priests.' Swallowing beer,
smoking, he stood and argued half the night.

At closing time he left so solemnly
you might have thought he went to meet his death.
She had hysterics on her wedding day
when she smelt lager on her husband's breath.

What Will You Do, Love?

'What will you do, love, when ambition presses
and from your caresses
I fly away?
Obliged to sever, I wonder whether
we'll feel together
day after day?'

'When I am alone and you are the apple
of the eyes of people
beyond my view,
I'll pray that praise will never destroy you,
I'll wait to enjoy you.
That's what I'll do.'

'What will you do, love, with concerts flopping
and no one clapping
your husband there?
If nerves or drink or rich fools tempt me
and my wallet's empty,
love, will you care?'

'If you come to bore me with a bad luck story,
love, I'll ignore ye
or break your head;
but, poor and pale, if it's honest failure
I'll see what ails you
and warm your bed.'

'And if in the nubile girls of fashion
I find a passion
that makes me stay,
what will you do, love, if I deceive you
and want to leave you
and stay away?'

‘The usual thing: with my young heart aching
but never breaking
I’ll think of you;
but the wounds will heal, and when grief is over
I’ll love some other.
That’s what I’ll do.’

Cavalier Lyric

I sometimes sleep with other girls
in boudoir or cheap joint,
with energy and tenderness
trying not to disappoint.
So do not think of helpful whores
as aberrational blots;
I could not love you half so well
without my practice shots.

A Man of Principle

Last night the wife was fucked into the ground
by a fat rugby player, both in a state
of silly drunkenness, their vile weight
hanging around my neck until I drowned
in disgust and fear. Foolish and ill,
lying, deserted on our double bed,
all night I watched them at it in my head,
inventing insults, planning to kick and kill.

But this bright day my wife's simplicity
and my good mental habits show instead
a glowing, well-pleased woman back in bed
beside me, kindly pleasured. I can see
no mark of evil on her nakedness.
Her aching breasts have only been well used,
were never prettier. Her mouth is bruised
but smiling. She doesn't love me any less.

These same good habits let me feel my way
back to the man she left me for last night
to see him human and to judge him right.
The light of reason turns night into day.
It's true my wife had had a lot to drink,
so had the man, and I. They wished to fuck.
She told me, said goodnight. I wished her luck,
then I grew sick; but I am cured, I think.

Goodbye, Sally

Shaken already, I know
I'll wake at night after you go
watching the soft shine of your skin,
feeling your little buttocks, oh my grief,
like two duck eggs in a handkerchief,
barely a woman but taking me all in.

I think our love won't die –
but there I go trying to justify!
What odds that we'll never meet again
and probably other girls will never
bring half your agony of pleasure?
Fidelity is a dumb pain.

God, but I'm lucky too,
the way I've muddled through
to ecstasy so often despite
exhaustion, drunkenness and pride.
How come that you were satisfied
and so was I that night?

It's true for drinker and lover,
the best stuff has no hangover.
You're right to spit on argument,
girl. Your dumbness on a walk
was better than my clown's talk.
You showed me what you meant.

Good mornings from every night
with you, thirsty and sore with appetite.
You never let me act my age.
Goodbye to all analysis and cause-
grubbing. The singer wants applause
not criticism as he leaves the stage.

We Belong Together

Only our misery is genuine.
Oh, let her have her way,
murmur, 'I'm yours. You're mine',
and save wrecking another day.

'A sweet exchange,' they say, but I hate
exchanges. I hate the brass throats
of brokers in halls where prices dominate
and love hangs, empty as their overcoats.

I regret even the childish marriage vows
we giggled in the face of Heaven.
The ghost of that contract is in our rows . . .
bargains are struck, bargains are driven.

For this philosophy I burn.
I am sick of love and my wife leaves
to consult a solicitor, to turn
my house into a den of thieves.

The Wife-swappers

I know my wife, or you for her, will say
she isn't just a factor in the pain
of others. Once I've got her out of the way
I'll feel her virtue and her charm again.

This is why husbands in the Sunday press
encourage wives to pose, to play at whores.
The extra cash is handy, but means less
than trapping them in freedom, opening doors.

They used to circle and evade us, stood
unique and dangerous, and even when
they smiled and lay beneath us, nude,
they still could dress and leave. They can again;

but my wife weeps with children in her arms
or leaves the house with iron in her soul
to hurt herself or do her husband harm,
not just to feel a strange prick in her hole.

It's people who believe absurdities,
who must, to feel secure, lock up their lives,
that in the end commit atrocities.
I play strip-poker with my neighbours' wives.

For

Have I become an old whore too?
It feels like it explaining to my far-out
nephew why to take the long view,
the virtue of playing safe when you're in doubt.
The argument is fool-proof: to eat
you must work; do it the easy way;
repeat what they tell you to repeat;
get in and through the university;
and *then* you can bargain, *then*
you can get an interesting job
and work from the inside. But when
is it ever safe to call a slob a slob?
Before that the nephew will be as rotten
as you are, his urgent truths forgotten.

Against

That was a sentimental one.
A fool-proof argument is true.
There's nothing to be done
if you don't *know* what you have to do.
In writing poems you don't invent a new
language. To do your own thing
you study what the older poets do
and find yourself by copying.
And you won't – you won't want to – change the nation
because you'll know how little you understand.
The best – the good best – is a variation
on a popular tune. A new heaven *and*
a new earth is either a daily event or not to be.
I am not Jesus Christ, and neither was he.

In Memoriam: Judy Garland

At forty-seven Frances Gumm is dead,
a plump, unhappy child who got ahead.

Towards the moon from her ecstatic face
notes soared. The moon is an awful place.

Discs are turning. Needles touch the rings
of dark rainbows. Judy Garland sings.

Stephano Remembers

We broke out of our dream into a clearing
and there were all our masters still sneering.
My head bowed, I made jokes and turned away,
living over and over that strange day.

The ship struck before morning. Half past four,
on a huge hogshead of claret I swept ashore
like an evangelist aboard his god:
his will was mine, I laughed and kissed the rod,
and would have walked that foreign countryside
blind drunk, contentedly till my god died;
but finding Trinculo made it a holiday:
two Neapolitans had got away,
and that shipload of scheming toffs we hated
was drowned. Never to be humiliated
again, 'I will no more to sea,' I sang.
Down white empty beaches my voice rang,
and that dear monster, half fish and half man,
went on his knees to me. Oh, Caliban,
you thought I'd take your twisted master's life;
but a drunk butler's slower with a knife
than your fine courtiers, your dukes, your kings.
We were distracted by too many things . . .
the wine, the jokes, the music, fancy gowns.
We were no good as murderers, we were clowns.

Censorship

A crappy bookshop in a country town.
The manager sets five soiled copies down.
He doesn't care what honesty is worth.
Indifference is a virtue in the North.

'This is pure dirt,' he says. I shake my head:
'It's true, it's funny, and it should be read.'
He says, 'We get schoolchildren in the shop,
and people have complained. We'll have to stop
taking your magazine if you print dirt.'

I remonstrate, 'Look, can't you see how hurt
young Harrison would be to hear you talking
like that about his work . . .?' but the man is walking
back to his lair. 'That poem will outlast
a wilderness of sermons from Belfast!'
I shout, and chase him, catch him as he darts
into his office, and grab his private parts.
He shrieks out, 'Jesus. Help!' I squeeze some more,
and two teenagers knock the office door.
We hear them whisper, 'Someone is in pain.'
Damn right. I squeeze his private parts again.
'What's wrong?' a girl's voice trembles. 'Christ! My balls!
He's trying to tear them off,' the critic calls.
'Shame on you, sir,' I whisper in his ear.
'Such language, when a young person can hear.'
'It's true. It's urgent. What else could I say?'

'That's how the poet feels,' I smile. 'Good day.'

Didn't He Ramble

for Michael Longley

'The family wanted to make a bricklayer of him, but Ferd. was too smooth and clever a fellow. He preferred to sit in the parlour out of the sun and play piano.' Henry Morton

There was a hardware shop in Main Street sold
records as well as spades and plastic bowls.
Joe, the assistant, had a taste for jazz.
The shop being empty as it mostly was
I tried out records, then, like seeing the light,
but genuine, I heard Josh White:
I'm going to mo-o-ve you, way on the outskirts of town.
Where was my turntable to set it down!
A voice styled by experience, learning to make
music listening to Blind Willie Blake,
walking the streets of a city, avoiding cops,
toting a cheap guitar and begging box.

The campus poets used to write of saxophones
disgustedly and sneer at gramophones;
but the word of life, if such a thing existed,
was there on record among the rubbish listed
in the catalogues of Brunswick and H.M.V.,
healing the split in sensibility.
Tough reasonableness and lyric grace
together, in poor man's dialect.
Something that no one taught us to expect.
Profundity without the po-face
of court and bourgeois modes. This I could use
to live and die with. Jazz. Blues.
I love the music and the men who made
the music, and instruments they played:
saxophone, piano, trumpet, clarinet,

Bill Broonzy, Armstrong, Basie, Hodges, Chet
Baker, Garner, Tommy Ladnier,
Jelly Roll Morton, Bessie Smith, Bechet,
and Fats Waller, the scholar-clown of song
who sang *Until the Real Thing Comes Along*.
Here was the risen people, their feet
dancing, not out to murder the elite:
'Pardon me, sir, may we be free?
The kitchen staff is having a jamboree.'

History records how people cleared the shelves
of record shops, discovering themselves,
making distinctions in the ordinary,
seeing what they'd been too tired to see;
but most ignored the music. Some were scared,
some greedy, some condemned what they hadn't heard,
some sold cheap imitations, watered it down,
bribed Fats to drink too much and play the clown
instead of the piano, and failed – the man was wise,
he did both painlessly. Jazz is a compromise:
you take the first tune in your head and play
until it's saying what you want to say.
'I ain't got no diplomas,' said Satchmo,
'I look into my heart and blow.'

What if some great ones took to drugs and drink
and killed themselves? Only a boy could think
the world cures easy, and want to blame
someone. I know I'll never be the same.
A mad world my masters! We might have known
that Wardell Gray was only well spoken,
controlled and elegant on saxophone.
He appeared last in a field with his neck broken.
The jazz life did it, not the Ku Klux Klan.
Whatever made the music killed the man.

The Straight Line and the Circle

for Billy Stokes

I was maimed on Everest
by a man like a boy scout.
The world is his now.
I count myself well out.
Me, the maker,
the broker, the breaker
of what? I used to swear
time was better
some place, somewhere.

As I explain and you sneer
I feel myself about to disappear.

Oldtimers remember me
for whom they turned their spars
and planks to skinny ships,
not for fishing, to travel
over horizons, unravel
ribbons of exploration.
Lighting out
for the territory,
for gold that never would be cash,
was what it was all about.

I told you ways to read
the bright jumble of stars
and find directions out.
Remember the fantastic
maps I helped you draw?
My bright transfers
on your minds unfurled
sails in all those harbours,

inflated names: The East,
The Indies, The New World.

I was alive in a gleam
only men get in their eyes,
in songs, in talk in taverns,
light years from their wives,
indifferent to the screams
of slaughtered animals,
the weight of power, the brute
work of policeman and prostitute.

Sight to their sleeping eyes,
a moon to those tides,
in smoky theatres of dreams
I showed my slides:
The Summer Palace at Peking,
palms on a warm shore, the smell
of spice, a wailing music,
women, a parchment plan
of the lost entrance to the Treasure House
under the orchards of The Great Khan.

Now men who never saw
the sea cannot forget,
thanks to ancestral memory,
the shape of an inlet
where long-boats scraped
ashore, the look of a cape
round which is Durban.

And all those great migrations
were mine, when a leader
turning, rearing his horse,

would nod, and whole nations
shouted with one voice
and moved forward.

From two miles up
I watched the millions
creeping over Europe,
bringing the groves of pillars
and the statues down
with their dream impetus.
Now I'll be dead soon.

You've scoured the round globe
in straight lines
till there's no room for doubt.
Our dreams are history,
and time will run me out.

It was all a game to me.
What else can it be?

Games were our life,
comradeship, love-affairs;
but now the world's your wife,
rear children, cultivate
community, responsibilities.
I feel like old Falstaff
who used to make that young
administrator laugh, fading
into the crowd cheering
the changed boy's parade.

Reformation leads to crime.
Better to talk in bars

till closing time.
A last drink, lad,
remembering all
the times we've had.
Think kindly. Don't call
time and the sea my
invention. I only lied
about a landfall.

For Jan Betley

The sad river passes
through melancholy glades
where leaves are silenced. It is late.

Under damp grasses
under the mist and trees, grenades
are stored in boxes, and will wait.

A God Judges

for Derek Mahon

1.
An instinct, useless and predictable
as toe-nails, has them at sea.
They launch thin yachts on this
and call it sport, though light craft,
fashionably painted, sink
as terribly as the *Titanic*,
with less pageantry,
and weekend sailors drown.
Merely to sit here quietly
is defiance, stripped down
to durable clothes, topped
with a dandy cap, beer in the cabin,
girls waving from the shore.
Between their knees a twisting beast
is held, a hand hangs in the mouth
of the sea, tingling like love.
You know a word of this
might never cross their minds.

If clouds smother the sun and the sea jostles them
the sudden face of death will be a surprise.
The knitted cap in the bilges, limp
as a drowned puppy, a powerful symbol
focused clear for a moment before their eyes.

With death for sauce, what appetites
they have for their spare hours.
Quiet and dignified, like *National*
Geographic photographs
of primitive tribesmen
or itinerant labourers,

these bank-clerk yachtsmen
carry their conquered fear
with balanced pride:
their trophy is themselves.
Above their dripping pints
precisely remembered weekends
run in their heads like ballads.
Their hands, grown hard and brown,
are more than keepsakes – evidence.

Holding worn tillers they have felt the sea
heaving a fraction of an inch of wood
away, a huge sky of moving air
trapped in the spread of elegant canvas. A god
judges their choice of ropes, the knots they tie.

2.
What are their women doing?
Neglected girls spit when they hear
Old Bull is dead, drive off unscathed
on mopeds, their wild scarves flung
behind them, in act, indifferent as the waves.

Mothers who smiled only to please
once too often, who used to tease
their green sons, laugh at their silly jokes,
broken connivers, who should have forbidden their children

to play dangerous, fashionable games,
ruin their teeth on sweets, smoke cancer sticks,
now weep at last and curse and tear
at their breasts, unpin their greying hair.

And yet, God save us, the silliest mothers
like the prettiest girls have business
in their wombs; under the nylon briefs
they are kin to Yoruba women and Indian squaws
who wait in exactly similar postures
for life to burst between their legs
wetting the grass or blankets with blood.

There's a time for hating lovers who are always elsewhere
when the nine months are up, on business or sport,
who make their entry with a proprietary air.

Photographs

Snapshots tell me nothing
about my father or anyone else
in my dead family. They all chose
to record unaccustomed smiles,
unusual highjinks, or
were merely abstracted
when the new machine eyed them,
offering communication to the future.

I am the same – my wife
and I are never glaring
in photographs. No one has caught
my fist raised to hit her
or her contorted face
vomiting hate, weeping.

Page after page we are smiling
or looking handsome and absorbed,
at the seaside, lying in hay,
clutching our marvellous kids,
having a marvellous time
against lovely landscapes,
the Antrim coast, the woods of Arcady.

Poems are different.
Strange what crossings out,
what concentration it takes
to be caught with my pants down.
Like Ulysses, holding evasive
Proteus by the throat
through monstrous changes,
flows of invective,

till he settled down,
I have to know to live.
So keep the camera on me.
I'll stop playing the clown.

Uncle Jack

In the first Great War my Uncle Jack
fought and only just came back.
To Derry, to the old homestead,
he brought war with him in his head.
When governments closed down their hell
he still kept waiting for the shell
that ruined his mind and killed his mates.
He raced along the parapet
screaming as though he'd never stop.
His soldiers dragged him off the top
and patched him up, not lame, not blind;
but shell-shocked. Everyone was kind
and helpless. He was never still.
He went to church and steeled his will
to sit like other men, but sweat
dripped off his fingers' ends and wet
his boots. They led him home again,
but every turning of the lane
hid snipers. Any sudden sound
flicked him face-down on the ground.
My mother's glad the Asian Flu
killed him. 'He was so much like you,'
she often tells me. Jack and I,
bookish, intelligent and shy.

Years after you had been betrayed
I grew up innocent and played
in fields and haysheds round the farm
you knew before you came to harm.
I liked the odds and ends one hears
of a dead uncle through the years.
I touched and smelt your uniform
but never dared to put it on.

The sort of tricks you used to do
for cameras are my tricks too.
I have this feeling that I owe
something that you will never know
to you, Jack – *my* life lived with care.
I'm older than you ever were.

Drowning Puppies

for Joan Newman

Their small pink mouths were opened
unnaturally wide
and little tongues stuck out too far
because of how they died.

I brought the bucket with its load
into the kitchen. There
the mother with her living pups
enjoyed the warmer air.

I paused before the Raeburn,
but the bitch saw nothing strange –
her master tipping rubbish
into the blazing range.

Epigrams

1.
Happiness can't marry, she only flirts.
Whatever you live with is boring or it hurts.

2.
Declining appetite
made him polite.

3.
When I had curls
I knew more girls.
I do more reading
now my hair is receding.

4.
Now that my faculties give in
I see the need for discipline.

West Strand Visions

The man alone at the third floor window
is the man alone at the cliff's edge.
Below him gulls are cutting each other's
invisible paths of flight. Bent sideways
in his cockpit above the dog-fight
alone he observes engaging bi-planes
locked in each other's sights and strategies,
diving, swerving and climbing heavily,
and droning earthward in flames.

The man watching the pony-girl waving
on the West Strand to her three assistants
and suddenly rearing her horse and wheeling
off at a canter, followed by donkeys
into the grey curtain of rain,
is the man watching barbarians gather,
Tamburlaine, was it, or Genghis Khan,
shaggy in robes strange to the watcher,
returned from reconnoitring,
deciding and acting on God's plan.

The man who watches neglected children
leaping in yellow light of sunset
by waters whipped by wind, majestic
ten yards out and fierce,
but gentle in the shallows,
is me, estranged from mystery,
trying to hear what they say,
envying no one in the world but they
who never use words like 'beauty',
shouting in apparent ecstasy
a pane of glass and fifty yards away.

The Younger Son

Natural strength and will
he had, to struggle through thorns
and all to find her room
in one continuous
ambitious movement.
And then he stopped.
Oh, she was beautiful
and so much more than just
asleep, so primly propped.

His body faltered. His mind
ran on to its reward.
From distant times, from fame
and mystery, her hundred
years of sleep, this girl
would rise into his arms.
Down the great stair
they would descend to marriage.
It was his life she would share.

His life? It had been stumbling
in her direction. And what
was she but beautiful?
Yearning for beauty had been
his youthful nature, his dream;
but now, to kiss, to create
a life and offer years
of variable bliss,
what people do in marriage?
The boy was kneeling in tears.

He found himself at a window
rubbing a hole in the dust
to look down on his world

where trees were vaguely waving
with modest signs of spring,
a bloom on the brown branches.
The pane was suddenly wet
with rain. Love was a smile
reflected on his face,
'I'm not dead yet.'

Just walk back to the inn
for peace and comfort, a meal
and a bit of crack with the maid,
and sup mulled wine
maybe, and read by the fire.
He could certainly do with a bath.
Below were the broken branches
and trampled grass that faintly
marked his heroic path.

Right then, a last look,
a tender touch, and goodbye . . .
but horribly he felt
his head bending, his lips
pursing to kiss. On contact
her body writhed with pain,
her eyes were open, her mouth
screaming, himself trapped
in a room trying to explain.

On Circe's Island

for Nell Dunn

1.
One day I found her summer house
most of the glass intact
but the wood riddled by worms,
the white paint flaked.
Age gives such character,
and an odour, strange and good,
of musty red geraniums
from my childhood,
some place where I'd been happy,
at peace to read
books my parents hadn't heard of
but I seemed to need.

2.
Apart from this I was relieved to be
abroad no more on the disastrous sea
that killed companions and servants and cast me

on wrong islands where curving white
sands and bays for shelter and other familiar sights
hid monsters too big for any man to fight.

What with the summer house
and Circe's friendly thighs
this seemed a paradise.

Then one day, lying out, lay next to mine
a familiar face, Joe's face, and yet a swine,
so I knew we were threatened. By magic this time.

3.
Everywhere's unreliable that isn't home.
In guilt I remembered my own wife and my son.
This stunning stranger kept me from my own.

There was always going to be danger being away,
enjoying idleness and novelty.
Destined for hard work and little pay,

I saw my great bow in the arms' store.
I thought, 'If Penelope stops watching the shore,
sweet lodgings are all I can hope for.'

4.
Circe's charm and humanity
and even her need were not for me.
One is not the same as another.
Responsibility must be particular,
not to every creature under the sun,
not universal love, but cleaving to one.

5.
But that is a moral truth.
My neglected self grows here. The crude
joys of fresh sex and high-class booze
are less than that ruined hot-house, the solitude.

6.
But, degrading my men could never be right.
I walked the perfumed sandhills at night

hearing my brothers grunt and scrape in the sty
while I, if the flesh moved me, was free to lie
on my lovely friend in her goddess's soft bed.

'Love me, love my men,' I said.
She grinned and changed the subject, but I stuck
to my point, refusing to chat with her or fuck.
I was stubborn, glum and moody and unfair.
This was a manly quirkiness to her.

7.
She didn't budge an inch till I raised my sword.
Then she promised, and was as good as her word.
Virtue paid out its bonuses all round:
as the boys lifted their forelegs off the ground
their human standing as they stood erect
was more than I'd remembered to expect,
and she had grace to see it was good too,
thereafter helping us with all she knew.

With her beside us hope seemed true at last.
'Wave your wand and waft us homeward, fast,'
I whispered, confident of my charm.
Aside, a little malicious, she took my arm,
'I see your future, being with vision blessed,
and there are more adventures to digest,
crimes to be expiated, chores to do.
No one is going to make it home but you.'

Nothing I could discuss with the lads. Again
it was father remote from son, master from men.
We stayed and sort of enjoyed ourselves a year.

And every day new virtues became clear
in Circe that my wife won't have. I will hunger
for her in time, so much sharper and younger.
Instead of thrusting home to love, I will grieve;
but the revelation is tied to the need to leave.

8.
That summer house, the walk there through the wood,
dusty geraniums, sun-warmed solitude.

Her little breasts, thin waist and crooked smile.
The sea of shifting hillocks, cold and vile.

My faithful and unlucky shipmates, friends.
My wife and son, my old age, journey's end.

9.
Joking and kissing, making plans in vain,
we ventured on the wine-dark sea again.

Robinson Crusoe

Before I left the island
        this book was in my head –
people must see you
        or you must tell people.
Man Friday hardly understood
        a word I said.
He walked in uninvited
        and sat down at my table.

He seemed to admire me greatly,
        my gun, my civilised ways,
then suddenly got bored.
        He might have slit my throat.
Nothing was settled between us.
        He would disappear for days,
then burst in, grinning,
        hanging on to my coat.

I will call it love in my book.
        The nearest word I can find.
When the vessel came to my rescue
        Man Friday had gone out.
I don't know why I wanted
        so much to leave him behind.
I crouched in a cabin waiting
        to hear his awful shout,

imagined him bursting through
        the trees, his gesticulations
from the receding shore,
        ignored by captain and crew.
Nothing. Escape. The intercourse
        of polite nations.
How sweet to know what one is,
        what one is trying to do.

Last night a bad dream took me:
        Man Friday had pursued
so fast he was in England
        waiting on the quay.
No one could stop his grinning
        impulse to intrude
into private things, upsetting
        all that is sacred to me.

Fear Test: Integrity of Heroes

for George Craig

Of those rebellions that we start in jest
some must be fought out in the open street
with barricades and possible defeat.
I shake with fear, but those days are my best.

Each time a chance of love is here
it seems her kids sleep in the room below,
neighbours are going to let her husband know.
Those are my best nights when I shake with fear.

Waiting backstage to sing, hating displays
of self, yet filled with songs
that no one knows but me . . . well, pain belongs
to birth, all births. I shake on my best days.

At last asking my silly boss to take
my resignation, getting off the fence
and telling him why. Who needs a reference!
I know my best days, but I always shake.

Good risks are those you hardly dare to take.
Who has a faculty for turbulence
and storm is sick; the healthy have more sense.
They have a use for courage when they shake.

That shock of horror when the way is clear!
I wish I had more stomach for a fight.
I wish I had panache – but I'm all right.
Those are my best days when I shake with fear.

The Second Coming

The end is in sight now. In the beginning
I had revelations, I was the reborn Christ
preparing to heal the world's fever with simple
truths and courage fit for the sacrifice.

Marriage changed me. The hero was ashamed
to fail to make one woman happy, I think,
to find himself nonplussed in argument,
lazy, impressionable, fond of a drink.

Now he is glad, with effort, to provide
food for his wife and children. He feels at night
like a glass globe sheltering the flame
of family, his little world's uncertain light.

He is a teacher, but all he hopes for now
is to get the students talking, coax the shy
and tease the pompous, help them to clarify
their indignation a little. I still try!

That soaring mind I had survives, locked
in its cabin, roaring enigmas for commands
at serviceable Simmons, the first mate
busy at what he seldom understands.

Flight

At that moment the mucous membrane slid,
under which bones and feathers were folded.
A muscle stirred and twitched on my shoulder knot,
a shape was growing behind me. The sun was hot.
With drying came distinctness, feeling extended
through to the tips of sailing wings that spread,
now huge and serviceable, overhead.
I was to pull them down, and they would try
to lift me off these stones into the sky.

The Ballad of Gerry Kelly: Newsagent

for Gus Martin

Here's a song for Gerry Kelly.
Listen carefully and see
what's the moral of the story.
It makes no sense to me.

Worked ten hours six days a week,
Sundays closed at three.
They say he made a decent living.
Rather him than me.

Social centre for the neighbours –
not much cash in that –
buying fags or blades or tissues,
waiting on to chat.

Sixty-nine the nightmare started,
Loyalist anger rose:
sweet-shops, butcher shops and pubs
were burned down, forced to close.

Who'd believe who never saw it . . .
the broken glass, the noise,
voices shouting, 'Fenian bastard'
– little Ulster boys?

Down the hill of lies and horror
Belfast city slipped.
Twice the Tartan thugs came for him,
robbed and pistol-whipped.

Standing in his shattered shop
and taking inventory

of loss and damage, Gerry Kelly
longed to get away.

Who would buy the ruined business
that he'd worked to build?
No one; so he waited, hoping,
until he was killed.

One dark evening last November –
turn the lights on till we see –
Gerry Kelly still in business,
wife gone back to make the tea.

Sorting out the evening papers
while his son is selling sweets,
in our time, our town, two gunmen
walk in off the streets.

Claudy

for Harry Barton, a song

The Sperrins surround it, the Faughan flows by,
at each end of Main Street the hills and the sky,
the small town of Claudy at ease in the sun
last July in the morning, a new day begun.

How peaceful and pretty if the moment could stop,
McIlhenny is straightening things in his shop,
and his wife is outside serving petrol, and then
a girl takes a cloth to a big window pane.

And McCloskey is taking the weight off his feet,
and McClelland and Miller are sweeping the street,
and, delivering milk at the Beaufort Hotel,
young Temple's enjoying his first job quite well.

And Mrs McLaughlin is scrubbing her floor,
and Artie Hone's crossing the street to a door,
and Mrs Brown, looking around for her cat,
goes off up an entry – what's strange about that?

Not much – but before she comes back to the road
that strange car parked outside her house will explode,
and all of the people I've mentioned outside
will be waiting to die or already have died.

An explosion too loud for your eardrums to bear,
and young children squealing like pigs in the square,
and all faces chalk-white and streaked with bright red,
and the glass and the dust and the terrible dead.

For an old lady's legs are ripped off, and the head
of a man's hanging open, and still he's not dead.

He is screaming for mercy, and his son stands and stares
and stares, and then suddenly, quick, disappears.

And Christ, little Katherine Aiken is dead,
and Mrs McLaughlin is pierced through the head.
Meanwhile to Dungiven the killers have gone,
and they're finding it hard to get through on the phone.

The Blessed Mary Hegarty

for Weldon Thornton, a song

I'm sitting at a paint-stained table
in North Carolina State.
Time should be running out for me,
but I don't feel too late.
So many well-fed people
would cramp your heart I know,
thinking of the scrawny legs and chests
on the kids in Ballinasloe.

First Chorus

> You are my little gold whiskey,
> you are my big black pint,
> I'd throw my life away on you,
> but that's not what you want.

And every pretty thing I see
I wish that you were here:
the Wild Plum and Forsythia,
the Quince and Flowering Pear.
I walk through Weldon's pinewood
and watch the small buds break.
The Dogwood and the Red Bud tree
I love for both our sakes.

Second Chorus

> I must not make you promises
> or use love like a chain,
> but embrace you and release you
> in ecstasy and pain.

The night I was kept from you,
waiting for the kids to sleep,

and my wife to go to *her* bed,
I wondered would you keep awake.
I got to you about half past two
and lay down by your side –
you had a flannel nightdress on,
so plain I could have cried.

Third Chorus

My heart is in a prison cell,
but the walls shake with its shout:
is this at last the one true love
we've heard so much about?

And sleep was all I wanted,
and I lay and held you tight,
and closed my eyes and waited
to be swallowed by the night;
but oh our tendril fingers twined
and you turned your mouth on mine –
at once we were the grapes, the growth
and the drinking of the wine.

Repeat First Chorus

It's Blake we're saying over,
about kissing a joy as it flies.
We've seen too many marriages
not to be scared of ties.
We don't expect contentment,
and there is no god to ask
that having found what we have found
that what we have might last.

Repeat Second Chorus

Oh Blessed Mary Hegarty,
my daffodils, my Spring,
young mother of my green-grass world,
my pale sea at morning,
my sheltered, whitewashed garden yard,
my shining rain-wet streets,
my scented phlox at evening,
my bed with linen sheets.

Repeat Third Chorus

Summer Lightning

Linda is the film star
who, to put it mild,
couldn't act the peasant girl
who drove the Justice wild.

She was scared of thunderstorms,
something made her sure
'heavenly electricity'
would be the death of her.

Lightning killed her mother,
she would go the same.
Crazy Russian peasant,
Olga is her name.

Justice's name is Russian;
Igor let us say,
played by George Sanders
who himself would slay,

saying that life was sordid –
but that is recent times.
This is an ancient movie
with two good lines.

To escape her drunken father
Olga marries slob,
then performs on Igor
an indecent job.

Fiancé sees them at it,
turns sadly away.
Surely this is travestying
some great Russian play?

Ageing roué, local count
is now bowled over.
'I want to be a Countess, Igor,
you can be my lover.'

Igor angry and besotted,
smeared by all he hates,
pleads to start new life together
in United States.

'Not America,' she cries,
'where everyone is equal.
Don't be jealous of the Count, dear.'
Then the tragic sequel.

Igor's lost his only true love,
Olga's ruined his life,
and now she spurns him. Angry Igor
stabs her with his knife.

Then her husband comes and finds her
in that lonely place.
Howling strangely, shirt-sleeves bloodstained –
open and shut case.

Justice Igor questions Olga
just before she dies,
surrounded by some magistrates,
focus of all eyes.

Surely Olga will accuse him.
'Tell us, how did you die?'
'Heavenly electricity
struck me from the sky!'

So she dies, and ruined Igor
lets her husband hang.
Then the Revolution
enters with a bang.

Old Order finished,
Igor morose and daft.
Old Count plays the violin
to his former staff.

Igor writes his story out,
old Count has a wheeze . . .
it must be a great novel,
might relieve the squeeze.

Takes it to a publisher
without reading a word.
The pretty publisher – you guessed it –
is Igor's former bird.

Draw the strands together:
Igor's wicked ways
symbolic of an order
that itself betrays.

Ex-fiancée wants to love him,
if only he'll confess.
Igor hasn't got it in him
to redeem the mess.

Runs in panic, hits policeman,
bullets set him free.
'Why?' a stranger asks him. 'Heavenly
electricity . . .'

Summer Lightning is the movie,
crazy Tzarist flings.
Storm before the real storm.
Stalin in the wings.

For Thomas Moore

When the young have grown tired
and the old are abused,
when beauty's degraded
and brilliance not used,
when courage is clumsy
and strength misapplied
we wish that our seed
in the dark womb had died.

But when youth finds its singers
and old men find peace
and beauty finds servants
and genius release,
when courage has wisdom
and strength mends our wrongs
we will sing unembarrassed
your marvellous songs.

Ode to Walter Allen

On sitting down to the big typewriter the distinguished author bequeathed to the English staff when he left Coleraine.

Walter Allen's grubby fingers
mucked up this typewriter.
His memories of drunken bards
made fading evenings brighter.

And even when I'd heard the stories
time and time before,
I loved them for the style
and for the way he held the floor,

one foot upon the hearth, one elbow
on the mantelpiece . . .
and then it was that night with Dylan
Thomas or MacNeice.

My spittle on a tissue poised
to wipe the dirt away,
I bless you Walter Allen
in the distant USA.

He smoked a chain of cigarettes
from morn till late at night.
I never saw him cadging one
or begging for a light.

He was prepared, capacious pockets
stuffed with twenty packs.
Unless he was provided for
he never could relax.

He neither fished nor mountain-climbed,
no swimmer he, no dancer,

member of one society alone,
The Friends of Cancer.

He read a lot and wrote a lot
and talked a lot, and drank,
and if he had, by God he earned
his money in the bank.

Poet, scholar, critic, he,
and novelist and smoker,
the scourge of sociology,
pomposity and poker.

He could be crabbit and evasive,
could be rude to bores,
hard on Hobbits and Mikados
and Vice-Chancellors;

but gratitude, the perfect butler,
wipes complaints away.
Grow sweeter, sourer, subtler, Walter,
in the USA.

John Donne

'There's more to style than honesty.'

When you lost touch with lovers' bare skin
how could the textures not get thin
in your verse? The real blood the fleas sucked
that sang through your and her veins when you fucked
was lost for God's magic bargain drops,
and life was teasing torture, nice when it stops.
Genius is tempted to ingenious lying,
to brazening out betrayal, justifying
such acts as that old interfering king
forced you toward. *You* could do anything!

After a brave attempt to marry free,
gaoled and neglected, you chose piety,
turned an encrusted back on sweet enjoyment
and – fuck you, John – made love to your employment
improvising belief after the fact,
acting in bad faith, living the act,
faking a hot lust for the Holy Ghost!
I dare dispute because I loved you most.
They'll say I want you to write more like me,
with truly liberal consistency;

but your young self, your verse, condemns defection
from the erection to the resurrection,
bullying congregations like a bawd
for Him, then grovelling. Gawd!
It was a difficult position,
like Galileo's with the Inquisition;
but he at least had grace to stay indoors
and not make weapons for the torturers.
You, having once made such a lovely fuss
on Love's behalf, betrayed her, worse than us.

Drunken Emily

for Eileen Mullen

Emily the secret drinker
holds her liquor well,
not a verse stain on the carpet
not the tell-tale smell,

the odour of spilt poetry,
the thrown-up metaphors,
empties stacked up in the cellar,
stumbles, farts and snores.

Orchard sunlight dapples shadows
where she sits asleep.
All, alas, is as it should be
when the neighbours peep.

Starched and spotless linen frames
an ordinary face,
little harmless hands are patting
false clues into place.

Once the family doctor wondered
if the face was false:
routine fingers, jarring, felt
the thunder of her pulse.

No one knew how far she went
till after she was dead.
We found her letters to the world
and wondered as we read.

Who supplied the potent liquor?
Have they found a still?
Will we ever make and market?
No. We never will.

Dickie Wells Said: Variations

1.
'It's only when the crowd deserts
the ballroom we play concerts,
missing the nights swinging and sweating,
serving the dancers in our true setting.
The change isn't our choosing
certainly. We know what we're losing,
we blow different somehow.
It's an imaginary music now.'

2.
In Derry we learnt to love before
we could talk, foxtrotting the floor,
nibbling earlobes
under the spinning crystal globes.
In the ballroom in Bishop Street
the educators of our feet
were James McCafferty's swinging
band and Mick McWilliams singing.

3.
I wish my lovely lucid songs
had the conviction Elton John's
get from just knowing they're wanted.
You have to be good not to be daunted
by indifference, to have the temerity
to play in empty halls for posterity,
for many a valiant old bore
insists on coming back for more.

4.
And of course the old jam sessions!
When work was over we eased tensions
entertaining ourselves and extending the art,
playing wild things, trying parts
we hadn't heard till then.
For the employed ones that was Heaven.
The unemployed were sort of sad,
all jam and no bread.

5.
We're only up here
to give your weddings atmosphere,
to help shy guests rejoice,
to find hidden feelings a voice.
As Jesus said, 'Stuff the applause,
we're here because we're here because
the rat race has gotta swing.
So let's see everybody dancing.'

For Imelda

There were no poems that year,
but every night driving from work
the red haws on the hedges
took me unawares, looming
in the milky car beams
as lush as cherries;
a sign they said of the hard
winter to come or maybe
the loveliest summer
in living memory,
my memory, my dear.

Meditations in Time of Divorce

for Michael Foley

Society Street: 1977

1.
The economics of marriage:

when alimony splits the salary
you're poor again, like a student
at forty-five, staring out
of your rented terrace house
at the grey pebble-dashed wall
of the Presbyterian Hall
always in shadow.
                                        All he can know
of sunset is the red bricks
of houses across the street,
when they glow.

2.
Like a poor student. Yes,
drunk with possibilities.

A Protestant, a pilgrim,
seedy environments suit him.

Ancient Ireland's monks and sages
had small houses, hermitages,

for the soul's dark night, for mystic trances,
not keeping up appearances.

In dowdy narrowness, not gloom
but music fills the sitting-room.

Call sitting-room and hall and yard
workshop and shelter for the bard.

The diner, recently the cook,
washes the dishes, opens the good book.

3.
Courage and rigour
obviate simony,
pursuing the wild game
through thickets of irony.

The free agent breaks moulds
and casts out remorse.
The sign and test of it is
old chores are blessed.

Behold the change-shaper,
now Ulster's leading
lighter of a fire
with screwed up newspaper,

a dishwasher of genius – see,
entranced over the cracked sink,
his hot water and Fairy Liquid
slide grease from cutlery.

Wife memory devises,
in table wiping and draping

dishcloths over taps to dry,
new spiritual exercises.

He is tempted to God-pose.
He intones, 'Life is good!'
and the best disciple's response
is to snigger, 'Platitudinous old pseud.'

4.
With twenty dedicated years
of collected tape-recordings
his mean shelves are crammed.
They have him by the ears.

Trivial rounds and common tasks
embellished and glorified
by immortal voices, taped 78s
of The Weavers and John McCormack, are all he could ask.

Gene Kelly singing 'Love is here to stay'
and Bessie, 'Gimme a pig's foot.'
Finney reading D. H. Lawrence
in Nottinghamese, Third Programme plays.

Devlin and Mary Farrell in *All that Fall*,
Pinter's mandarin tribute
to 'Mac', Scofield as Lear.
How right he was to record them all!

This is his church. Rising from our dirt
we cross ourselves, crossing the street.
The aisle is full of strange noises
that give delight and do no hurt.

5.
A metallic siren wakes him now
for work, as the wife used to.
Unhelped, unhampered by once-loved
facilities, he rises on will power
and takes in the emptiness
that surrounds him, the narrowness,
the strange proximity
of mass-produced metal windows.

Lacking curtains so far
he must content himself to see
the wrecked backyards. It used to be
broad skies over the Atlantic,
white wooden bathing houses
on the bent wall of the harbour, a great
crescent of sand, gull cries.

Nevertheless he feels potential,
not loss. Like Saint Patrick he rises
reciting, up to his neck in cold
comfort, in good faith embracing
necessity, constantly singing, not
putting a sour face on it.

Alas for her the change is deprivation,
hence acrimony and divorce,
seizing the house-beautiful, the car,
the kids, lacking other resource.

6.
On the rocks he has to flower,
a sort of back-street merman

singing weirdly of a landlocked family,
left and remembered painfully.

He never enjoyed luxury; but, oh,
rearing a family, however unnatural,
was sweet: the dwarf night-garments
by the fire, scented with talc,
children's daft creative abuse
of language . . .

Penelope swooned
towards her father, offering all herself
outstretched to be carried, crying,
'Lakalady, lakalady!' and, hoisted up
on his shoulders, rode more like a lady
than any he ever knowed . . .

Conducting now from a distance
his cheques and good wishes fly in the post,
he is glimpsed occasionally, a ghost
at outings and once-off celebrations,
a presence beyond the television's glow;

but ruefully invigorated,
at home at sea, hated only
out of grief, loved, lost,
looked for from the big windows
occasionally.

7.
I will never go back.
They will not come to me;

but laughter, worried expressions
and quirks of personality

like voices on the wind
penetrate occasionally
to my soul and scar me.
That I must seem unkind!

Twenty years is a long time to play
at marriage; but all my gardens
went to seed, all our houses
decayed in my tenancy.

8.
Coleraine centre,
the Latin Quarter
imagined by Ulster lads
of the Fifties,
where Henry Miller,
the master of cliché,
Fitzgerald and Hemingway
were young writers in love with a city
that left them free,
living cheaply, accepted,
their Olivetti portables
on worn tables at window shrines,
white paper our only luxury
marked by prose sentences

as fresh as the croissants
and unwrapped vegetables
our girls carried graciously
singing up the stairs.

If youth is wasted on the young,
wisdom is wasted on the middle-aged
if we don't have the wit to do now
what we always wanted.

9.

He discovered an almost rural way
to walk to work yesterday
across the cemetery.
His father is buried here
and he loiters looking down
on a small desolate empty
arena with black marble walls.

Instead of meditating on death
he finds something to do, kneeling,
clearing a few square feet of weeds,
secure in dreams of a good
future that will come true.

Today, taking the same way
to work, there are plants on a wooden bench
for sale outside a shop.

He arrives at the grave
with a brown parcel spilling clay.
Fingers, not often calloused
by spade work, poke holes
for the frail roots of flowers
and press the earth home gently.

All smiles, in solitude, constantly singing,

he can relish the graveyard tap running
the black clay off his hands coldly.

Dirty fingernails all that day
will remind him. At desk and at lectern
two gesturing hands will convey
a personal message: 'I have knelt to honour
my father's grave, the ashes of my ancestor.'

On Sunday he brings his mother who smiles to see
her prodigal son rejoining the family.

10.
Surprised by joy –
to make this day complete
at midnight he hears knocking,
his girl walks out of the street

unexpected,
a half bottle of Powers
in her shoulder bag.
They sit till all hours.

Her only jazz musicians
have been Mingus and Coltrane.
When he plays her *West End Blues*
she asks to hear it again.

They drink the pure gold whiskey
and listen and talk.
It seems there is nothing they try for
that doesn't work.

She has a good job and enjoys it,
so they set the alarm
and drift to sleep in silence,
her head on his arm.

One night they were still kissing
when the dawn broke
on the ruined backyards,
a lugubrious joke

it seemed, in their joy,
Victorian spectres
of poverty, to scare *them* –
the board of directors!

Eden

He threw them out and slammed the gate shut
for what He found them up to. He was scared
like all angry people and unprepared
for love. He decided to blame it on 'that slut'.

Morally hung over He walked the walls,
straightened His stone picnic-tables, stared
sickly at the new padlock and the guard's sword,
waiting to welcome repentant prodigals.

If only they'd argue, face to face; but no.
They sneaked back to pick up a radio
left in a secret place in the undergrowth,
aimlessness their element they were loath
to risk losing. They drifted into the night,
relieved in every way to travel light.
The unprejudiced world was what those two lacked,
and of course they avoided the huge pathetic back
of God. To this day He is standing there,
banished. There *was* a world elsewhere.

After Eden

His last glimpse of the former wife
is after midnight, woozy with drink,
on a quick foray for old tapes,
and the front door is open, as always,
out of their shared instinct.

A ghost in his own shadowy hall,
the stairwell echoing still
with bitter shouting and slammed doors,
up in his old study he opens drawers,
and descends, his thieving arms full.

A man comes out of the kitchen and disappears.
At the car the wife grabs him, hissing abuse.
Hunched awkwardly, unloading his loot,
his high-pitched voice whining, 'Christ,
you've got everything else!' – he breaks loose,

'Look! We agreed . . .' 'I agreed to nothing!
It was *you* walked out on *me* with your whore!'
When he hits her, precious tapes unreel
and roll on the pavement. Again they are sharing
intimate touch – her nose, his knuckles, sore.

Will the long marriage never be over?
Love she would call what drives her now to close
fiercely against him, drinking his anger,
shameless and righteous, fronting
her husband, embracing his futile blows.

His last glimpse is of her standing
in faded chiffon nightwear, humble, beautiful,
like a dark harvest etching, *The Last Gleaner*,
a woman, lit by a street lamp, winding
tangles of gleaming tape on a plastic spool.

The Honeymoon

Remember last summer when God turned on the heat
and browned our bodies, remember how hard and sweet
were the green apples you bought.
Remember how quickly neglected nipples were taught
to take pleasure in kissing. Remember your sunburn peeled
after a day on the grass of the hill field
and the painless scars evoked a principle for us,
that the truly lovely is truly ridiculous.

A beauty like you can look sometimes dumpy and fat,
knock-kneed, hen-toed, and none the worse for that,
for when you recover your splendour suddenly
what seemed like flaws is personality.
The world has examined you closely and found you right
and beautiful with a more piercing sight
than fashion editors know. You thought I meant
evasion, a left-handed compliment,
but now know better; being able to talk to you
like this is love being true.

Nothing could get us down those days together
but lust, on grass, in mountain streams when the weather
was hot as ourselves, on collapsing sofas, on floors,
in the steamed-up Datsun in the great outdoors.
Our best man swore you would be black and blue,
and, true enough, love's frightening. You do
violent-seeming things; but no one's hurt,
playing by the rules. We rise from dirt,
stink, struggle, shining, having suffered nothing.
No wonder they say that God would have us loving.

The worst debâcle was, once, trying to screw,
erect, me knees-bent, on my feet, and you
tiptoe on Dickens's *Our Mutual Friend*.

No joy. Abashed, we thought it was the end
of something; but no, failing is all right,
a sort of roughage to the appetite.

Our strangest luck seemed, first, not good, but ill –
me slow to come, you inexhaustible.
That turned out well. I had not thought God's voice
was intricate and humorous, like Joyce's.

Even your tears, after our first quarrel
when you got strangely thick and I got moral,
were not exploitive. Remember our briny kiss?
Nothing was broken, nothing was amiss.

Cloncha

1.
On their first quest
they followed an impulse of hers
thirty miles North and West
in search of an ancient cairn
some other boyfriend
had shown her, shared
with her.
                    Relentless
she was with details,
tactless and true.
And yet he smiled,
learning and liking, and said
securely, 'I love you.'

'Stop! This is it.'
He stopped the car. 'No.'

He reversed six times
or more up narrow lanes,
harried by neck strain.

At last they asked a woman
who pointed over fields
to three high crosses,
standing (also patiently),
heavy with lost authority,
worn smooth, shapely,
landowners once in Ulster,
speechless now, gracefully
letting themselves be stroked.

2.
Exploring delightedly
as lovers do
(shoddy their workmanship
as it is in all
of God's creatures)
they congratulated each other
on the view.

Sunlight and wind that day
brimmed the broad plateau
of Inishowen with air
like tinted water, submerging
every colour but yellow.

In petal and bloom of benweed,
gorse and dandelion,
bright yellow intensified.

White mist blurred
the edges of stone outcrops,
branches of willows,
sycamores, thorn hedges.

3.
Modern poets and business families
live for their holidays –
Longley in Mayo, half
literary Ulster in Ardara.
Our hero's Arcady was here
with the bleak moors and strands,
for forty years near enough,
the Derry hinterland

between Foyle and Swilly,
from Malin to Buncrana
to Greencastle to Shrove,
Moville and Carndonagh.

The Anglo-Irish boy adores
broken demesne walls,
empty condemned cottages,
moorlands littered with boulders
gold-braided thinly with lichen,
sheep's wool coarse and grey
from Lear's theatrical beard
on the rusted barbed wire,
the dried-blood red of rust,
the fragile brilliance of fuchsia
dancing dolls, a Japanese theatre
in country hedges grown native
and deserted like Yeats's plays,
pale water agile on slatey beds
of mountain streams, rain
on hotel windows, the pale gold
of whiskies set on the wine-dark
wood of country bar counters.

Today he searched for anecdotes
to establish his rights there,
retailed his mother's world of Moores,
Montgomerys, The Royal School,
Raphoe, where young Magillicuddy of the Reeks
boarded, the names of her father's
two friends, Peter Sauce and Dorby Toye,
the aunts from Manorcunningham
who wouldn't inherit
a moneyless Scottish title,

Cunninghams, Rentouls, Kings, Craigs . . . .
Nothing of this was his or him.

All he could offer honestly
was a private childhood, secrecy,
a boy drifting alone through fern
forests and alder groves, smoking
his first woodbine above Carrig Cnoc,
a consciousness apart from ancestors
and local inhabitants, a stranger
at home in the present moment
happily, then as now. He was luring
a girl near his heart in this
occupied country of his. His voice
touching another, the singer's art.

4.
Truthfully he was ashamed
to be so much older,
too gratefully holding
beauty and youth.

Happy noises were going to be hollow,
however lovely she was,
if he wouldn't hear clearly
when the talk was callow.

But the feeling was there.
And what he learnt was this,
that what they felt was made
by what they were.

The value of love makes lovers

easy to scare.
In fear of loss, in fear
of opinions of others,

they lift weapons of jealousy;
bribe, bargain, threat.
Hard to accept time alters.

It has not altered yet.

5.
You've seen girls in the newsreels
running out of ruins
in ecstasy to embrace
an army of liberation.

A good moment in war.
The crazy celebrations
tell you how bad things were.

He didn't care who
set him free. He couldn't
do it himself, deadlocked
in bleak resistance,
hopelessly intimate
with his enemy.

Of course the girls step off
eventually. The battered
soldiers roar away.
In the free town
people may turn ugly.

There's not much that divides
armies objectively;
but you'd have to be very doctrinaire
not to fling your cap in the air
on days of liberation.

Peace grows out of war
grotesquely. Remember Stalin,
the liberator, and Eisenhower.

But Auschwitz is out of business;
Paris, though expensive, is free.

In private affairs
is less brutality.

6.

Well, this was one more lover's quest,
lovely, neither first nor best.

They had to question whether
their love could last forever.

Contentment always says
something like promises.

The years from war to war
must be worth living for.

I sing of natural forces,
marriages, divorces.

The Imperial Theme

1.
Girls werc of course strangers
to a man. We explorers
wheedled intimacy, pretended
ingeniously to speak
their language, exchanging
bright cheap beads of fantasy,
words of love, for delectable
cuntland, free trade and grazing
on breast and belly, rest and shelter
in forests of perfumed hair.

We coaxed lust from these
placid animals, preaching
a heady gospel of free love,
bargaining words of tenderness –
these tribes were starving –
then firing parting shots
into the herd, watching them
stir, stampede, rustling off
a few head.

I must admit we worked best
drunk and in darkness.
I never relished the blackened
fireplaces, slumped figures
weeping in the light of day.

2.
The loveliest country
in the New World
was your pale smooth belly
with that tiny pond

southward,
and the slow descent
to sheltered scrubland,
the hidden cave
with its weird formations,
vagina, clitoris, explained
by laws of nature.

Outside, after,
the whole climate
was filled with sighs
as we leant smoking
against sheer walls
of white thighs.

At the back of my head
I felt your eyes
following me
all the way down,
blessing my journey,
crying small cries
of horror
and encouragement.

Knocking On

The more I wear glasses
the less well I see.
Mary at the study door
was hazy to me,

hard on eyes to look at,
hard on mind to grasp.
I panicked and slammed on
my spectacles fast

and lost her, rightly,
for glasses are grotesque,
like the ache in my elbows,
the pains in my breast.

Love is for the young ones.
Even if they're not
elegant or gentle
their blood runs hot.

After experience
we measure our resource,
the pulse beats softer
further from the source.

Intricate and careful,
too fond of style,
even the nicest girls
turn away to smile.

Cuchulainn at his last post,
Sweeney in the trees,
hands out of plackets
and off plump knees:

I should seek, with those men,
the danger and the wet.
Pull back the sheet, love,
soon, but not yet.

Olive and Davy

When conversation failed
the family album came down.
A portrait of Auntie Olive
in her BA gown

stunned me, hair sculpted
neatly round her ears,
so beautiful I stole it
and had it for years.

When age and her last illness
ravaged her face
the gold hair still shone
with all its old grace.

I remembered it last night
when Uncle Davy died.
Was that why he wanted
no one at his side

this last year, a widower?
We knew he'd seen more
of the wide world than most of us,
Australia, Samoa,

Nigeria; but not much,
we presumed, of life,
him with his speech defect
and his lovely wife.

Uncle Davy, very quiet,
and Olive, my Aunt,
so strikingly beautiful,
so gay and so fluent

his one rebuke in public
echoed like a riot,
telling his lovely back-seat driver,
'Olive, be quiet.'

The winter she died
he brought sweets and sherry
to my mother's bridge evenings
and got mildly merry.

We hardly broached his bottle:
but always next time
he brought the same parcel,
courteous and kind.

Suddenly he grew, it seemed,
impatient for death,
and symptoms followed, pallor,
shortness of breath,

a new, old man, Davy,
blank, impolite,
preferring no company
night after night

to neighbourly solicitude,
an idle rout
trying to perk him up,
eking him out.

He died. This is an old story
from the common stock:
an old crock longing
for another old crock,

longing on beyond youth,
beyond beauty's decay,
beyond the grave – so it seems –
for Olive, Davy.

From the Irish

Most terrible was our hero in battle blows:
hands without fingers, shorn heads and toes
were scattered. That day there flew and fell
from astonished victims eyebrow, bone and entrail,
like stars in the sky, like snowflakes, like nuts in May,
like a meadow of daisies, like butts from an ashtray.

Familiar things, you might brush against or tread
upon in the daily round, were glistening red
with the slaughter the hero caused, though he had gone.
By proxy his bomb exploded, his valour shone.

The Old Woman of Portrush

The tide ebbs on a grey winter shore
where I used to lie in the sun
roasting my lithe soft body
that now is shown to no one.
From cold ribs of sand
rises a dank exhalation.

The wrinkled hide of an old woman
covers what I was (what I am),
slim, pretty, sophisticated
Kathleen ni Houlihan.

Look (don't look) at my sagging hams
that once would blithely lift and open
for tennis players and film stars
and great singers. I am heartbroken.

But I haven't a bad word for the men
whose fingers combed my light, tight curls.
It's my own daughters I can't stand
and disrespectful eyes of girls.

Men's promises were lightly spoken
and lightly heard, for love was free
among the rich and beautiful.
Only time has ruined me.

Even the sunniest days here
are little comfort to the old.
Our scrawny, ailing flesh and limbs
wince equally from heat and cold.

Giggling little chits
chase security.

After a brief fling
they want a tidy house
in a housing estate,
and a wedding ring.

What will never blaze again,
inside me an ember
glows teasingly,
miserably, a dull pain.
Does any man not remember
his nights with me?

Even the wanton youngsters now
are ignorant how to love and live.
What pleasure do they have themselves?
What pleasures are they fit to give?

We trained ourselves like samurai
or ballet dancers or athletes,
and then came forth to shine with grace
in the world at large and between the sheets.

My men drove powerful little cars
fast, with the lightest finger touch,
devouring the miles to Dublin,
calm and amused and loved so much.

Stiffly I stalk the promenade,
so fearful of the buffeting sea,
I who could face love's rough and tumble,
fine-boned and naked, fearlessly.

That harbour once held two great yachts.
Ladies with diamonds at their throats

danced with the navy and military
where now are skiffs and fishing boats.

I drank champagne with toreadors
who fucked me stupid through the night.
Now with retired dames I doze
in the TV lounge's frigid light

and glimpse old lovers on the screen,
ghosts, like myself, of former glory,
in minor roles, old generals
and fathers, eking out the story.

A bony old fool calls for me,
so lined, and such an awkward lover,
stiff in the leg. When we dine out
we drink too much. We loathe each other.

My great four-poster's a warm island.
Outside are the silent corridors.
My windows shake in the winter storms.
The cold attendant ocean roars.

Lament for a Dead Policeman

His wife
My love and delight
the first day that we met
in King Street in Coleraine
I knew I'd never set
eyes on your like again.

You courted me a year
but did you ever doubt
that I'd have married you
before the week was out
if you had wanted to?

Though you dug with the wrong foot
for me you were all business
buying our hillside plot
on the Garvagh Line, for me,
raising the roof beam high
in a grove of oaks, for me,
the Sperrins a far smudge of blue.
My dad, the plumber, for me,
set gleaming basins and a bath
and a shower and fancy taps, for me,
working in spare hours
for free, like you, for me.

Old friends and institutions
made generous contributions.
My Uncle Tom, the joiner,
made cupboards, and a farmer
lent us his rotavator
to break the soil. A slater
worked evenings on the roof,
as if to offer proof

how much they all admired,
love, you who inspired
respect the way you served us
better than we deserved.

My memory lingers
on that spring day
you first approached me,
erect and smart
in the dark uniform
your family hated.
Who'd blame your pride,
the little strut in your step?
'Lord of the by-laws,'
I said. With one hand lifted
you slowed a speeding
lorry or moved on
a noisy drunk
or a bunch of rowdies.
Big head inclined,
you listened to old ladies
courteously. You laughed a lot
then, straightening us all out
in your dry Derry way.
You never seemed too hot
in your heavy overcoat,
or drenched in persistent rain,
belt and cap shining,
black truncheon and revolver.
Approach me again tonight,
lighten my dreams, lover.

Many who didn't like you,
impatient of the law,

held you in awe. Their shifty
eyes, their raised fists
fell, seeing your stature.
I thought while you were there
order and law would hold,
we might endure forever;
but, sweetheart of my soul,
one day of sheer bad luck
a little mixed-up thug,
with a gun in one hand
and a bun in the other, shot you.

My hero and my friend,
father from Londonderry,
mother from Maghera,
you never flattered
lawyer or magistrate,
J.P. or barrister,
however loud they could be
or condescending. You knew
the law as well or better,
in spirit and letter served it.
That was your source of power.
You never deviated
and were well loved and hated.

My dearest honey,
at our home tonight
what can I answer
Francis and wee Tom
when they ask for Daddy?
I wiped the blood
from our front door
with lukewarm water

and Fairy Liquid.
Your gore I swabbed,
darling, as you would
have done, my true one.

Sweet love, good father,
I thought so clever
you might dupe all danger,
I can hear their footsteps
still and the doorbell.
You lowered the paper
in our sunfilled kitchen
and caught your coat up
on your finger as usual
and drained your coffee
and sauntered the hall
idly to answer.
Like a stick in a biscuit tin
guns started.
My world caved in.

Your people want to wake you,
but that is not our way.
When you joined the police force
and not the IRA
didn't the whole bunch hate you?
Knowing what they condone,
they might as well have killed you.
Let them get off the phone
and give us peace to grieve you
that honour what you've been.
There will be tea or whiskey
for old friends who drop in.
Though God knows I want no one.

Nothing could lift this gloom
but you to wake and hold me,
my dear, in our own room
where I have put the children,
just to be less alone.
I will get in beside them
when everyone has gone.

His sister
Brother, I'm still ashamed.
Your whole life was lamed
from taking the hard bribe,
forsaking your own tribe
to live for an ideal
so simple and unreal,
the abstraction 'law and order',
when Ireland with a border
mocks a far older law
as all your kinfolk saw;
but you were super duper,
an Ulster Gary Cooper
for whom integrity,
elections, democracy,
were the first word and the last,
not the outrageous past,
the lies, the blatant slander,
prejudice, gerrymander.
You were the family's pride,
and we were mortified.
Tame Fenian, they would pat you.
Dear, they were laughing at you.

And still and all
we want to wake you.
I rang the bitch
you stooped to marry.
She was too busy
or too tired.
A private funeral
and no wake.
Have they no feelings?
Her husband dead
and her sleeping.

Most of the crowd
you once knew
are in the States
or on the broo;
but we'd see you right
for one good night,
a decent wake
for old times' sake.
We'd drink a last
toast to the best
outside right
ever from this estate.

His wife
Sister she may be –
I couldn't reply;
but I'm heart-sorry
it wasn't I
answered the doorbell
or ran before you
to face the gunbursts,

to gulder, to beg mercy
or gather the bullets
in my dress or my flesh,
to save you, any way.

But how could that be,
my law enforcer?
It was your place to face them,
mine is to mourn you.

Your racing pigeons
in the shed are fluttering.
Your two greyhounds
need exercise.
I will walk them myself
with the old leads
your hands wore shiny.

Strange sight, a woman
striding at twilight
behind dogs, mind empty.
The unnatural fruit
of murderous politics.
I am thinking of nothing
but your life-blood stiffening
your green shirt front.

Marrying you
altered my heart.
Another good man
maybe another day?
I keep that thought
away, unnatural.
What those wee skitters,

those sick teenagers
with gun power
and creepy ideas,
did is pure evil.
Even my children's
sweet bodies against me
make up for nothing.
I'll rear them well,
aching and empty.
It is weedgrown,
our old bower,
and our little stream
is almost dry. Oh, Tom!
Goodbye.

Stone dead upstairs as you are,
I still expect the patrol car
to call to pick you up. You seemed
so much at the centre. You scanned
the papers for signs, you tossed
in your sleep with worry. They will be lost
without you, decisive and so terse
and clear. Things are going to get worse,
although these last ten years
we have spent counting murders
of friends and colleagues,
old men and other Teagues
(we called them 'forty-niners'),
the retired or part-timers,
the easy touches, the ripe fruit,
though many times a new recruit,
a boy in a Land-Rover, was hurt
or blown to bits by a mine in a culvert,
remote-controlled. How much you hated

remote leaders who manipulated
the young impressionables, the unemployed.
And what was the phrase got you annoyed?
(You said, 'The smoothest drivel's the worst.')
Violence has reached an acceptable level.

The slickness of the media sickens me,
the tone of the questions of TV
reporters, their phoney sympathy,
fishing for widows' tears.

My face is trapped there in the news,
contorted, breaking with intimate grief
beside the grave, at every fireside.
Could they see I was proud too?
But they never want the whole story
or follow it through below the surface.
The viewing audience might get bored.

Your black cap sat on your coffin
on the British flag you served so well.
There were lines of bitter confused colleagues,
praised and abused with loaded voices.

There was an older man in tears:
'If they'd untie our bloody hands,
let us alone loose in the ghettos
and root the bastards out. We know them!'
I could hear Tom answering, 'Aye,
fair enough if we go by the book.
You can't enforce the law breaking it.
What's half broken is broke entirely.
Remember, that was the Bs' mistake.

'The distinctive feature
of Irish life, politically,' –
he could spell it out rightly –
'isn't just bigotry, it's the easy
toleration of violence by any side,
moral confusion, tearful cruelty,
acceptance of crime becoming collusion.'

It is spring now.
Our garden is lovely:
daffodils, primroses,
simple and bright.
Listlessly weeding,
the sap-flow and singing
sharpens my longing.

I know no waiting
can change this aching.
My husband is dead,
my bed is empty,
my heart is sore.
I suppose you can hear
nothing. Every gesture
is waving goodbye
at thin air.

If I knew what to do
that hasn't been done
I would do it:
letters of protest,
a march of the women
to Stormont or Dublin.
I would spend time
and money, mortgage

the house again
and sell the car,
join with the Peace Women
or anyone to break through,
to find a policy
to draw diehards and wreckers
inside the law.
But who would I speak to?
Jim Prior or Gerry Adams,
Paisley or John Hume
or Molyneaux?
They are only repeating
themselves, point-scoring,
and I've nothing to say
except what you said:
'There's a law there
to enforce and to obey.
If you want to alter it
there is a lawful way.'

One more policeman dead
matters to very few. That's
a change from better days. The dangers
they go through daily, wives and children
terrified, justify high wages;
but worried him too. 'We're still
getting recruits, but who?' Tom said.
'What they say goes on in Castlereagh
might very well be true.' Maybe
he's better out of it, uncorrupted.

I've stopped crying. A bad-
tempered, good-looking woman
with dark eyes stares back

at me from the mirror.
Her husband, the policeman,
has gone into the night
for the last time,
able to help no one,
he lies stiff and useless,
off duty forever.

An Irish Epiphany

Always after the martyrdom
the chip vans arrive.
In the free republic merchants
and visitors will thrive.

The Catholic Church's Revenge on James Joyce

The brightest of bright scholarship boys was made
in their own image, powerful, fluent, afraid
of exposure and contact; but to such a degree clever
he knew those suave expounders could never deliver
the good. When Nora Barnacle laid her hand on
his fly, simply he found himself Christ's son,
and, of course, the message was what it used to be
of clear love and the blessed ordinary.

The most democratic of writers found to hand
techniques he was trained to. The message must stand
in a towering Gothic prose cathedral,
the stained-glass shepherd scarcely visible.
Those bastards had to be shown! His work must tower
over the countryside! So the people cower
coming near his creation and sidle in, astounded,
and wait for official experts to show them round it.

Elegy for Two Students I did not Know

Adventuring down on the rocks after a disco –
power is fascinating – two students risked the waves,
and that foam-robed Vice-Chancellor in rut,
en route, drunk as a lord, laughing, roaring
in his own wild career, jostled them.
Slave of the winds that blow, who
he was taking in he did not know.

Children, whatever your plans were or queries,
affairs of love or learning, your nice quirks
of personality, over them great salaries
and golden handshakes pour coldly, coldly.

Children, is this not what they told you?
What were you learning from literature and science?
You ought to have listened harder to make sense
of our solemn mouthings, grasped our indifference.

The Farther Shore

The hotel extends, neighbours enlarge their garage.
I bought this house for the view of the sea,
and year by year it is narrowing on me.
The diminishing prospects of old age!

There's an old phrase from the hymnal, 'the farther shore',
and that's what I call that distant inch of white
shining across the lough. There is often sunlight
on Greencastle Strand when all is gloomy here.

When the minister promises life eternal my face
glowers involuntary. Heaven forbid
I should linger on, a passionate woman, hid
in this wrinkled old aching carapace.

This isn't complaint. My mind is brimming always
with childhood, children, grandchildren; but I want no more
of the good life God gave me. The farther shore
is a real place where we spent our holidays.

The Harvest is Past

'The harvest is past' is painted on tin
in crude script and hammered in
to a small tree at the end of our road.
It shadowed our entrance to this happy abode
and may, I suppose, be there when we go.
I would like the local prophets to know
their ancestors built us a good home,
that my eyes harvest this ample room,
my son's pine shelving, the tiled floor,
this vase with berries, this drink I pour
to toast our anniversary. Let them know
that most of the things we plant grow,
that problems keep pushing us towards solutions,
that the way of the world is revolutions,
that our common noises are laughing and song,
that Imelda is pregnant, that they are wrong.

So Long Lives This

A branch of red berries,
cut off the gusty bush
at the shed's end, glows
orange on my writing table
for a week or more, still
now and unbending, stuck
in our pink delft jar.

In tumult it steadies me,
a shrine, a statue, familiar
in every detail. Indoors
only the leaf backs show
that once sheltered the berries
from the winds that blow.

October in the Country: 1983

What you can suffer you can sing.

Wind shakes my window frames
with an empty afternoon roar,
and that damned born-again Christian
is out riding his lawnmower.

His garden is cluttered with Dormobiles,
powerboats of glossy fibreglass,
hedgecutters, rotavators, vans:
the expensive hobbies of a pain-in-the-ass.

And the farmer whose cowshed spoils our view,
whose poisonous leaking silage destroys
blackcurrant bushes and rhubarb clumps,
whose presence is always stink and noise,

is pumping his foul slurry and racing
backwards and forwards to his fields,
mechanically incontinent
in hot pursuit of higher yields.

We hear his crammed uneasy cattle
shifting and groaning in the barn all night
in winter, heads stuck out through bars,
up to their knees in their own shite.

This is my refuge, my countryside!
Yet, believe it or not, to speak the truth
I am happier here in my middle years
than ever I was in my Derry youth.

The only material for jokes
is annoyance. The cruel course

of our human race has been fixed for us
democratically: damned at the source

but improving, maybe. I give my vote
to reformers: but setting the cattle free
and driving them south to the Sperrins? No.
We'd be caught, and cattle frighten me.

I have lit the fire and closed the shutters
against noisy gardeners and farmers.
The votive light in my amplifier
draws me to worship great performers.

For Janáček

Don't argue with growing the only way
out of what you were dropped in, local clay;
but it's not that easy to honour
your own impulse, to know your hour
is coming as sure as you're not shouting
for recognition. Don't shout. Sing.
And when they're applauding you, bone
idle and beautiful, be still unknown,
the Muses blowing down your throat.
Name and address are of little note
so long as you're sure you do, or will do,
the work no one knew you were born to.

The Pleasant Joys of Brotherhood

to the tune of 'My Lagan Love'

I love the small hours of the night
when I sit up alone.
I love my family, wife and friends.
I love them and they're gone.
A glass of Power's, a well-slacked fire,
I wind the gramophone.
The pleasant joys of brotherhood
I savour on my own.

An instrument to play upon,
books, records on the shelf,
and albums crammed with photographs:
I *céilí* by myself.
I drink to passion, drink to peace,
the silent telephone.
The pleasant joys of brotherhood
I savour on my own.

Home from Norway

a fantasy

After the long journey at last I lie,
head on my girlfriend's tits, and tenderly
she asks what poetry I've brought from Norway.

There has been so much! We last met weeks ago.
Images tumble out, she hears me ramble
of jewelled woods, bright veined stones, mosses that glow,

maples so red they have surely a blood taste,
shimmering birch foliage, feathery,
like cheese-cloth festooning the tree's white waist.

The dark-robed firs' boughs' gestures are priestly,
disapproving. They recede precipitously
up, up, as far as the eye can see.

Bleak and twisted rock is the Troll's Wall.
Hell is above us in black mountain and sky;
Paradise, ploughed fields at the foot of the fall

and the painted wooden houses. The moist light
of Norway washes bright those encrusted woods.
Water is falls and cataracts, all white.

The still water in lean fjords reflected
small fields and tidy farms. The walls of rock
above them threatened rather than protected.

Within was enough warmth and comfort and dry
piles of split wood for the cast-iron stove.
Colours of October leaves and cloud berry

were woven in rugs that hung on varnished pine.
The stove and walls and the blond wife glowed.
She was saying gently, 'I am his and yours and mine.'

Our duvet, stuffed with duck feathers, was light
and voluminous, floating on three bodies, white
to the neck, then red with weather and blushing. Aquavite

in a bottle and milk in a jug on the table
flavoured our kisses. I waked to the dry rattle
of bells out in the rain on necks of goats and cattle.

My hosts were city people at their country place.
The locals were stocky bodied and bumpy faced.
Only on skis and skating they discover grace.

This is the country of Amundsen and Nansen,
gentle and healthy explorers and good fun,
listeners to strangers, harmers of no one,

and brave Thor Heyerdahl of *Kon Tiki* and *Ra*,
whose voyages embody – even if little good
comes from those scholar ships – sane brotherhood.

My girl's fingers furrow my greying curls
with ointment for an old sore. Buttered farls
and Spanish coffee she brings, and asks about girls,

'Were there any in Norway that pleased you as much as me?'
unbuttoning her silk blouse to show me the lacy
anchorage her globed breasts ride in, and I see

the soft valley between, my favourite place.
My neck base is hers. Her face brushes
against it. I am home and dry. 'Welcome,' she says.

Ulster Says Yes

One Protestant Ulsterman
wants to confess this:
we frightened you Catholics, we gerrymandered,
we applied injustice.

However, we weren't Nazis or Yanks,
so measure your fuss
who never suffered like Jews or Blacks,
not here, not with us;

but, since we didn't reform ourselves,
since we had to be caught
red-handed, justice is something
we have to be taught.

Honeysuckle

1.
Pale candelabras of soft honeysuckle,
creamy, crimson-streaked, tangled
in the stiff intricate hawthorn hedge.
Such powerful fragrance gathered
these country girls to tease out blossoms
one at a time, adorning each other
in the creamy half-light of summer,
crimson-streaked. Girls sauntering home
in flower print dresses
after a late dance, they probably spread
breathless and giggling across the road
as Austin Murphy accelerated.

He was drunk, in a lousy mood merely,
punishing all that horsepower.
The girls would have waved after his car
if they had heard in time. Wherever it be
he has lifted them into eternity,
Eileen, Bridget and little Maeve,
chasing each other lazily.

2.
Cigar in his teeth, drink on his breath,
smell of burnt fat in his hair,
inside his head the rattle of dishes
and an insult from a customer,

angers of ignorance and ambition,
a joke that didn't go well,
and whisky after whisky. He wasn't a man
driving his car home, but a missile.

How could the girls resist him?
Dresses and flesh went first,
spines and ribcages were splintered,
lungs and hearts burst.

He raised them all for a moment
like high spirits, and let them down,
limp in their finery, cuts and bruises
like bright jewels, and drove on.

Blood was dissolving their necklaces
of straw and blossom, found there
like a pile of rubbish in the morning dew,
an odour persistent in the air.

He staggered down by lunchtime
looking as usual for a cure,
his head not really splitting.
He saw his gardener from the door

wiping bent headlights, clearing
the bumper of honeysuckle and straw,
and was incensed at the impudence:
'Ye have done it this time, sor.'

Dandering

I think the cow wanted my daughter to touch her
as any mother would, deprived of her young.
Her beautiful wobbly pale teats hung
in the air. Her nose, touching the metal bar
of the gate, was square, pale and wet.
My daughter didn't want to know how it feels.
The thin bony tail lifted, and shit
was oozing over her sex down to her heels.

Anna liked that, 'Popo,' she said, 'Popo.'
I practised voice on the cows, content:
'Four score and seven years ago
our fathers brought forth upon this continent
a nation conceived in liberty . . .' I see
to be always practising makes me a sort of baddy
exploiting my child and the beasts who gather naively.
Anna rebuked me, 'The cows are laughing, Daddy.'

Enlightened self-interest is a policy.
We both like level-crossings and the train.
She learns to stand back from the cars that thunder by.
If I stop for a smoke she watches a daisy chain
grow in my hands. She has learned dexterity
climbing the gates I lean on. I name it, and hand her,
a docken leaf when a nettle has stung her knee.
Now she invites me, 'Come on for a wee dander.'

Exploration in the Arts

An interviewer made the thrilling case
for Modernists: 'They were exploratory!
They made it new!' He brought a blush to my face,
for my own work's all song and story.
'To enter the jungle you really have to invent
techniques! To discover you have to experiment!'

Entering the jungle of what is and is not said
needs guts and talent and experience
to go as deep as Eliot and Pound did;
but let us stay this side of common sense.
Shakespeare and I and Byron and Brecht and Burns
offer ourselves as entertainment, turns.

Old Tom and Ezra battened on the old.
Making it new, my arse. Rapists! Damnation!
Where's the originality, the gold,
when every memorable line's quotation?
'Hast 'ou seen but white lilly grow . . .' The cheek, the gall!
Compare Pound's bits with the original.

ELIOT & POUND, industrial complexes, tower
in academe. Entrepreneurs, they bossed
and forced fashions that gave them power.
Writers like Edward Thomas, Hardy, Frost
didn't leave industries behind them. No,
they left a land conserved where things still grow.

Imperial explorers (at the best
brave and ingenious) only opened doors
into the happy gardens of the West
for bloody Jesuits and Conquistadors.
Greed was their basic right to interfere,
exploit, contaminate a hemisphere.

Undressing (transitive, intransitive)
is the only method. Savour the cooking meat.
Listen and watch precisely as you live.
Look up old recipes. Sit down to eat.
Use ancient forms, the journey, the family curse.
Use farce and tragedy. In the trade immerse.

That frigid crazy pair confessed too late
that what they'd conquered Grub Street with was lies.
Their final years were barren and desolate,
though Eliot warmed to what he'd satirised,
someone to dance with. Well, they weren't pathetic.
God knows they were both bright and energetic.

Tonight I'm hearing Beethoven discovering
depths in himself, trying to outplay
Bach, in his Hammerklavier. The ring
of challenge sorts down to humility.
The best are awed by what they've taken on . . .
imitator, pupil, companion.